Data Warehousing

Data Warehousing

The Route to Mass Customisation

Sean Kelly

JOHN WILEY & SONS

Chichester · New York · Brisbane · Toronto · Singapore

First printed in hardback 1994, reprinted 1995.
Paperback edition with revisions, February 1996.
Reprinted May and October 1996, January and March 1997

Other Wiley Editorial Offices

John Wiley & Sons, Inc., 605 Third Avenue,
New York, NY 10158-0012, USA

Jacaranda Wiley Ltd, 33 Park Road, Milton,
Queensland 4064, Australia

John Wiley & Sons (Canada) Ltd, 22 Worcester Road,
Rexdale, Ontario M9W 1L1, Canada

John Wiley & Sons (Asia) Pte Ltd, 2 Clementi Loop #02-01,
Jin Xing Distripark, Singapore 129809

Library of Congress Cataloging-in-Publication Data

Kelly, Sean, 1960-
　Data warehousing: the route to mass customization updated & expanded
Sean Kelly.
　　p.　cm.
　Includes bibliographical references and index.
　ISBN 0-471-96328-3
　　1. Industrial management—Data processing.　2. Decision support
　systems.　3. Corporate planning—Data processing.　I. Title.
HD30.2.K457　1994
658.4'012'0285—dc20　　　　　　　　　　　　　　　　　　　　　94-8497
　　　　　　　　　　　　　　　　　　　　　　　　　　　　　　CIP

British Library Cataloguing in Publication Data

A catalogue record for this book is available from the British Library

ISBN 0-471-96328-3

Printed and bound in Great Britain by Redwood Books from author's camera-ready copy

To Nicola, of course

Contents

Preface

This book is intended for information systems professionals and business users of information systems alike. My purpose in writing the book is: to analyse the role of information technology as a driver of corporate strategy formulation; to specifically address the history and relative failure of existing information systems to deliver real decision support capabilities; to examine the technological and architectural options which are available to remedy these deficiencies; to introduce and explain the concept of the 'data warehouse' and to explore the political, design and technological obstacles which may obtain in the task of transforming this concept into a reality. The term 'data warehouse' was originally coined by W. H. Inmon who has published some of the seminal material on the technical art of constructing the data architectures required in a corporate decision support system.

This book, on the other hand, is not focused exclusively on the technical agenda of designing a data warehouse and addresses a wider canvas which seeks to explore the 'What?' and 'Why?' of the data warehouse rather than a technical tutorial on the 'How?'. In this respect I have spent a considerable amount of time in exploring the patterns of development and utilisation of existing models for decision support systems in an attempt to place the data warehouse in context. In addition a good deal of effort has been expended in examining the implications of developing a pan-corporate architecture and the justification for embarking on such a venture.

A key message in the book is that the data warehouse in the essential technological vehicle required to slice and dice the market into the micro-segments that will enable mass production industrial organisations to transform into mass customisation customer-focused businesses. The data warehouse is not a new information technology application which will impact the standard business model—it is a new information technology architecture which will act as an agent to fundamentally alter the model of industrial production.

Corporate data which may be utilised in a wide range of decisions is stored in vast quantities in software applications which created this data. At this local functional level this data is well understood and meaningful for the purpose of the application. However, there is now a requirement to view all of the corporate data in a holistic fashion, i.e. to see the totality of the data in the enterprise constructed into integrated patterns and pictures which can add dramatic value to decision making. It is increasingly imperative for businesses to identify trends and patterns in data and to draw business conclusions from the behaviour of the data about the behaviour of customers, employees, suppliers or competitors.

The concept of the data warehouse has now been taken on board by virtually all of the leading hardware and software vendors but is still at a relatively immature stage in so far as no integrated product set or 'shrink-wrapped' solution is yet available. This book is dedicated to providing a coherent conceptual framework for such systems and charting a course for organisation is embarking on the corporate data warehouse journey.

Business people no longer accept the meagre quota of information which is output as individual by-products of individual transaction systems. Neither are they satisfied with the enormous volumes of data which they are offered in place of the information. Now they are demanding systems dedicated to the decision support operations of key knowledgeworkers.

A number of different concepts are explained in the course of the book in order to provide hooks from the software concepts to general business trends and these ideas, in themselves, are in no way novel or original. Because it is the intention of the book to synthesise these combined phenomena the high-level treatment of many of these items is necessarily superficial.

The guiding mission of the book is to provide practical assistance, within a coherent conceptual framework, to organisations which are committed to the goal of transforming their data into information of *strategic significance of the enterprise.* 'Transforming data into information' is a slogan which has become so overworked that the real meaning of the concept has been obscured. It is this author's contention that only a few dozen corporations world-wide have actually derived strategic advantage from analysing the patterns of their corporate data. This book provides a putative map drawn from the practical experience of the author and the shared experience of many of the other pioneers in this field. The modest claim that I make for this book is that, like all such maps, it is left for those navigators who may follow as a guide to some of the perils which they may encounter in the sincere expectation that it will shorten their journey and in the sure knowledge that it is incomplete.

We are now leaving the era of *Automation* and have embarked on a journey of *Information.* There is, as yet, no clear destination nor even an identifiable event to mark the distinction. What *is* clear is that the data warehouse is one of the first landmarks to be encountered in the new landscape.

Sean G. Kelly
Dublin, 1994

Acknowledgements

There are always in endeavours such as this one an array of people who are deserving of thanks and acknowledgement. To the many who facilitated me in my work and research I offer my heartfelt gratitude.

The few who were closely involved, in various ways, in the endeavour of actually researching and building the data warehouse I wish to identify here.

Many great people at (what was) the Teradata Corporation and now at NCR, but especially Carol Whittaker and Peter Rix. Hugh McDaniel and all of his colleagues at the Carleton Corporation. Tony Joyce and his colleagues at the IBM Information Warehouse Solution Centre. Paul O'Connell at Sequent Systems and Phil Codd at Ingres. John Rankin at the Index Consultancy Group for recommending that such a system be built. Bill Inmon for coming to Dublin to review the project. Ted Russell at Ernst & Young for teaching me how to build an enterprise model. John Boughner at US West in Denver for demonstrating what a data warehouse could actually achieve.

At Telecom Eireann I run the risk of being guilty of unforgivable omissions. But here goes. Michael G. Ryan for his courage and vision in sponsoring the project. Des Colman for always keeping a weather eye on events. Eamon Boland for representing the business users. Seamus O'Friel for his sheer enthusiasm. Tony Butler for hours of dialectics, and especially Kevin Nolan and his project team for building the bloody thing.

_____ Thoughts on the Subject

On the automation of knowledgework . . .
'The single greatest challenge facing the managers in the developed countries of the world is to raise the productivity of knowledge and service workers . . . this will dominate the management agenda for the next several decades.'
—*Peter Drucker*

On the utilisation of data to support decisions . . .
'The main objective in war, as in life, is to deduce what you do not know from what you do know.'
—*The Duke of Wellington*

On achieving quality through data . . .
'Eagerness to collect data will lead to a clue to the solution.'
—*K. Ishikawa*

On the value of information . . .
'If you had complete and totally reliable information on everything, then you would not need to do any thinking.'
—*Edward de Bono (from 'Masterthinker's Handbook')*

On the necessity for information . . .
'Whereas hydrocarbons were the major fuel for the industrial economy, information is the major fuel that provides energy for the new economy.'
—*Stanley M. Davis (from 'Future Perfect')*

On the ubiquitous computer . . .
'It has been a momentous change. Information Technology is no longer a business resource, it is the business environment.'
—*The Econonomist, June 16th, 1990*

Chapter 1
A General Introduction

It is probably a truism of all planning or control actions to observe that managers do not make decisions which are either *good* or *bad* but that they make decisions on the basis of good or bad *information*. For it has always been the case in military, political, commercial or civil endeavour that the quality of available intelligence is the key ingredient which determines the quality of any decision. Never was this a more compelling truth than in today's commercial world which is changing faster than the ability of decision makers to comprehend and analyse the plethora of data which is available to them. But what is not readily available to decision makers is the single succinct piece of accurate information which is required by them at any given time.

A commonly used, if somewhat trite, definition of 'management information' is "the right information in the right form at the right time". The source of most frustration in businesses is the inability of computerised transaction systems to generate management information which meets the requirements of this definition. Much of the data which accumulates in transaction systems is not easily accessible or has a meaning which is subtly (or significantly) different from what is required by the business or assumed by the user. Or the information is presented with too much detail, too little detail, covers too short a timespan or is generated at inappropriate intervals. Therefore, it is manifestly not the *right information*.

More often, the data required to support decision making will come from a number of different systems which are resident on a variety of different technologies. Providing this information, if it can be done at all, can only be achieved by skilled computer professionals who are not generally available at the whim of business managers. Therefore, the information is not generally available at the *right time*.

If the data is extracted, merged and converted into some kind of meaningful information which meets the requirements of the decision maker, very often it cannot be made available in a usable format. Typically the decision maker will have a relatively low level of computer knowledge and will want the information loaded into a particular spreadsheet package or other PC software tool with which he/she is familiar. When a printout weighing ten pounds is dropped on someone's desk it can be assumed that there is a good chance that the information is not in the *right format*.

The dilemma created for the corporate information technology department by these demands for data is centred on the difficult task of attempting to control the amount of scarce information technology (IT) resource being consumed by the insatiable demand of the business for information. Each time a report is generated by the IT department and analysed by the business it leads to an immediate demand for three further reports to illuminate the insights gleaned from the first report. The extract programs required each time are generally unique and very often have very few re-usable components. The interaction between the sea of information and the decision maker is generally a constant voyage of discovery for the latter. For the IT department it is an intolerable strain. This strain is the result not only of the effort required to specify, write and test the query program but also of finding suitable time to run the program against a production system without impairing online response times.

The response of the corporate IT providers (and a good deal of the international IT consultancy effort) has been to employ more and more rigourous methodologies, in order to comprehensively capture the information requirements, when designing new systems. One of the key objectives of these methodologies is to align the IT system with the business goals and requirements. This, in itself, is a welcome development in software engineering but the techniques employed, however rigourous and successful they are in capturing the *process* requirements, fail completely to capture the *decision support* requirements. The reason for this is that the business users complain, quite reasonably, that they cannot know all of their requirements for information in advance of the operation of the system. The true reporting requirements are only identified through the dynamic of the business process. It is necessary, of course, for transaction systems to be rigourously specified in advance. Most business transaction systems are, after all, the intersection between the organisation and the customer. These systems should *not* be a voyage of discovery for either!

The evolution of information systems has been charted from the era of Electronic Data Processing (EDP) with its operational focus on *automation* to Management Information Systems (MIS) which is producing some information but with a strong focus on *control*. The latest stage has been Decision Support Systems (DSS) which are addressing the productivity of knowledgeworkers by aiding less structured decision making.

Somewhere in this model of the evolution of information systems is the assumption that each successive wave of computing obliterates and replaces the previous one. And it is this assumption which seriously distorts the validity of the model. Clearly the wave of automation has all but passed and it is equally clear that those systems dedicated to decision support will attract the bulk of *new* information systems investment in the next decade. But the DSS systems will not replace the MIS systems for the DSS systems will be entirely dependent on the MIS systems and the data generated by them. For the foreseeable future both environments will co-exist with the investment in the automation of processes (online MIS systems) levelling out and the data generated by these systems populated onto a data warehouse which will provide the architectural basis for the development of DSS systems. This tendency is illustrated in Figure 1.

To build an effective DSS environment it is necessary to consider the need for a hardware and software platform where the corporate data conforms to the three necessary requirements for DSS development. Firstly the data must be integrated (with other internal corporate data). Secondly, the data must be enriched (through integration with external data). Thirdly, the data must be available (and not constrained by machine resource). To meet these requirements implies that the enterprise must dedicate a *separate* hardware and software platform to the task.

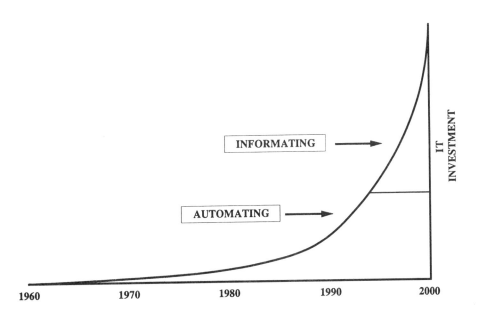

Figure 1 Information technology investment trend

The significance of data as a source not just of *operational control* but of *operational strategy* has been the key driver in the concept of the data warehouse. Operational strategy may seem a contradiction in terms and is an attempt to describe the need, in a competitive and turbulent market, to continually innovate and re-align strategy within timescales too short to be comprehended by strategic planning in the conventional corporate sense.

The frustration of computer users unable to access data has led to a significant IT trend in the 1980s -- independent user-led IT initiatives at departmental level. Unfortunately, the advent of the departmental computer has not been an unqualified success. What has happened here, perhaps unsurprisingly, is the emergence of multiple computers in different departments generating different versions of the truth distiled from the same data. In any case, in order to get the data on to their local systems, the business users have found themselves as dependent as ever on the IT department.

What is perhaps poorly understood in this respect is that data is inert and that, in itself, it does not confer any particular benefit on the business enterprise. Information, on the other hand, is a guide to action. This is a useful way to distinguish between the two since the main characteristic of a useful item of information is that it will trigger an event. Because of the paucity of information in organisations many managers have made a fetish out of collecting data in the forlorn hope that eventually, if they ever get the time, they will be able to discern in the data some useful pattern. The collection, analysis and storage of data tends to develop its own momentum and the volumes of data being held by organisations have proliferated to an alarming extent.

The crisis of information technology generally within organisations is currently reaching an apex and is driven by criticism of the productivity, the cost, the lack of integration and the lack of flexibility of existing information systems. Chief Information Officers (CIOs) who reached the top table of executive influence in the late 1970s have now, in many corporations, been banished back to technical obscurity. The centralised hegemony of the IT function in information system matters is all but dead. In the world of hardware and software suppliers, the turmoil is even more evident. The hardware has got tremendously powerful over the past decade but this power has been soaked up not by more powerful and functionally rich system software but by more user- friendly application software, especially in the area of presentation interface graphics.

While software has become easier to use, the way in which systems are designed and built has not changed fundamentally in the past two decades and the world of software development is not the welter of change that many observers believe it to be. The recession, the competitive intensity, open systems, computer-aided software engineering (CASE), downsizing and other factors offered as reasons to explain the turmoil all manage to sound like peripheral factors impacting on a more fundamental crisis. The efforts of the software providers have been directed at providing incremental improvements, more integrated product sets, more open products, utilities to simplify software construction and tools to re-engineer existing systems. The fundamental question, 'What do we do when everything is automated ?' appears only now to be engaging the attention of the industry when the stage has been reached in the history of information technology where virtually every business process in the developed world is already automated. It has been widely demonstrated that, since the nineteen-sixties, the productivity of managers, knowledgeworkers and service workers generally has been static or actually in decline. Given the enormous investments made by service companies in information technology, this paradox is not easily explained. Some of the explanations which have been offered lack credibility. For example, it has been suggested that not enough of an investment has been made in people and that the benefits have been absorbed by an increasingly complex environment or that the benefits are more quality than productivity oriented.

One of the key deficiencies in the policy of automation was the overwhelming concentration on business processes. The office was regarded by the workstudy analysts and later by the software engineers in the same way as the factory which they had just finished automating. If it moved, it was computerised. But not if it pondered. The challenge of supporting decision making was only satisfied at an operational and functional level by 'canned' reports which were spewed out of the transaction systems at week-end, month-end etc. Very often, this data was 'bad' data since it may have been too old, or too detailed, or too aggregated or un-integrated. Using 'bad' information generally leads to a worse outcome than using no information, since ignorance is generally a basis for caution. The task of devising strategy (through information and decisions) was divorced from the task of executing strategy (through business processes) and this artificial situation allied to the fragmented progress of automation ensured that information technology never fundamentally threatened the existing organisational culture. Now that the frenzy of automation is over, the real productivity benefits of the systems may finally be realised through integration and information.

The data warehouse is part of the response of information technology to the question, what do we do next? Like many innovations in technology it is a term used to describe a disarmingly simple concept but one which, over time, has the potential to evolve into something more complex and significant. What the data warehouse represents is a recognition that the characteristics and usage patterns of operational systems which are there to automate business processes and the characteristics of decision support systems *are* fundamentally different but that each environment is symbiotically linked to the other.

This in turn leads to the conclusion that the design differences as well as the problem of resource contention makes it impracticable to run both kinds of application against the same single image of the data.

Therefore, the data warehouse concept is about *unbundling* the two environments. In one environment the business automates its processes on many different online transaction systems in the most effective and expedient manner possible. The data from these many and varied systems is then used to populate a database comprising all the data necessary to support decision making in a separate data warehouse environment. Intellectually, the concept is not in any way challenging. Technologically, some interesting challenges are encountered and these deserve full exploration. But the key challenges arise from (a) determining whether the benefits which would accrue to an enterprise from having such a system would justify the cost and effort employed in such a project and (b) in assessing the impact of such a system on organisational culture.

Data is a strategic asset of the enterprise, perhaps the only genuinely unique asset which cannot be replicated by competitors. It is a true source of competitive differentiation and is, in most cases, located on cartridge tapes and stored in the dark caverns of the corporate data centre; and it is only retained at all because of accounting and company law regulations which require businesses to retain transaction data for a prescribed number of years.

Data is a by-product of business transactions and, like waste material from manufacturing processes, is disposed of at the end of the process. Well, the news is that the waste by-product can be re-processed. This will not be done in the online transaction processing environment which probably spawned the data in the first instance. Instead it will be necessary to construct a separate re-processing facility which will be dedicated to large-volume complex processing. This complete separation of operational update activity from the read-only data warehouse eliminates the locking problems and resource contention problems which are inevitable if it is attempted to apply extensive queries to production environments which have high update activities. It is simply a reflection of the optimum use of available technology to solve pressing business demands for both high-performance online processing and high- availability data access for decision support.

The data warehouse is a *subject-oriented* corporate database which addresses the problem of having multiple data models implemented on multiple platforms and architectures in the enterprise. The data warehouse is specifically attempting to address the challenge of corporate decision making which is having to happen in ever shorter timescales and which is having to include ever broader horizons. And the data warehouse is a response to the cry of help from the business users who are isolated on different islands of computerisation in the enterprise and who are demanding, amid acrimonious disagreement with one another, one single version of the truth.

In the world of industrial production there is now an environment of rapid and unpredictable change. Some of the most revered sacred cows of management science are mortally wounded. For example, it is the optimisation of capital, not labour, that is now the route to increased productivity. And flexibility now confers more advantage than scale. Mass production is giving way to the customisation of goods and services. Autocracy in the workplace is giving way to participation. At the same time there is a relentless process of international standardisation. Driven by competitive, regulatory, ideological and technological factors, all management practices, tools and techniques are converging globally and so too are the product offerings. The only fundamental source of competitive advantage that remains is strategy. The most likely battlegrounds for strategic advantage will be in market planning and in product innovation. The weapon will, undoubtedly, be information.It is likely to be found that a truly valuable item of *strategic* information informs the decision maker in a general way about the *totality* of a situation. this concern with the organic unity of the data from which the information is derived is central to the emergence of the data warehouse concept. Good information is the product of inputs from many sources and will, like good art, have in each of its parts something of the other parts. Unfortunately, the nature and evolution of information systems has meant that the quality of the particular has taken precedence over the quality of the whole. And, despite the fact that each particular software application is itself a quality system and can readily produce a profusion of particular detail the combined body of corporate information systems does not generally result in a unified whole. Where attempts are made to provide a unified corporate picture it has tended to be through synthetically combining summaries and aggregates in order to provide an 'executive view' of the data. Most often, this 'executive view' is combined from the many particular systems but is not connected to any of them. Behind the summary presentation of the data lies a void beyond which resides the disjointed range of operational systems into which the user cannot further navigate.

Therefore, it is the goal of the data warehouse to re-integrate the data in order to solve the problem of unity without surrendering the possibility of complexity.

As well as commercial evolution in the developed world there has also been significant technology-related social evolution. The vision of 'information superhighways' being discussed in the United States today includes ordinary citizens among the users of the vast network of systems. Undoubtedly, members of the public will want to interact with information systems in order to trigger transactions to buy, sell and consume products. But more significant, over time, will be the requirement of users to access packaged information. And finally, like the business users, the time will come when individual citizens will tire of the restrictions of shrink-wrapped information and will demand the freedom to directly interrogate the data on the basis of their own unique requirements.

One thing that has hardly changed at all in recent times is the manner in which investments in computerised systems are evaluated and these continue to be based on the premise that a *manual process gets automated* and in return the business enjoys the benefits of *lower operating costs*. This crude and simplistic 'quid pro quo' is ingrained in management consciousness. Investing in a dedicated decision support system requires a different mind-set because the basic proposition is different. The data warehouse type investment is based on the premise that an *intellectual process gets informated* and the business enjoys the benefits of *increased revenue or improved strategic positioning*. Many players in business and in IT are finding the transition from tangible inputs and outputs to intangible inputs and outputs too perturbing to easily come to terms with.

However, not all of the travails of commerce are going to be eliminated by providing universal access to integrated information; but the concept of a data warehouse facility separate from operational systems will be central to an amelioration of the current information technology crisis and these corporate decision support systems are likely to survive for the next decade and will be a key source of competitive advantage. In the fullness of time more advanced technologies will support a more conceptually elegant solution where transactions *and* queries can co-exist in the same computing environment against the same image of the data. But this nirvana is so far distant that any inclination by an enterprise to wait it out is likely to expose that enterprise to such sustained attrition by informated competitors that their position will become untenable.

And as competitive pressures intensify internationally the demand for sophisticated information grows and the computer industry is responding with early faint signals indicating a response. The response will not be a response to the challenge in technology alone but will require responses developed on a combination of technological, architectural, methodological, and visionary planes.

In the past, users have been given data access tools that did not work, were told to wait for new systems which did not deliver, were lectured about failing to specify their reporting requirements and were told to wait on new technologies. The term 'decision support systems' has been used to describe the next wave of software systems which are designed to assist knowledgeworkers to make better decisions and has been applied loosely to an amorphous range of systems. Most decision support systems have been conceived, designed and developed as problem solving systems. The assumption is that a problem exists for which there is an optimum solution and that the decision support system will safely navigate the user to that optimum decision. Now this is all very well if the problem consists of diagnosing a medical or technical condition or determining the stress levels of a structure or establishing the amount of material required to complete a project. But it is only in a very artificial and sanitised world that this could be represented as the stuff of corporate decision making. In the real world of corporate decision making there are no neat and elegant problems to be solved; it may even be true to say that there are no problems as such. What does exist are threats which the manager is constantly attempting to anticipate and avoid and opportunities which the manager is continually attempting to identify and exploit. The decision making paradigm does not conform to a 'problem-analysis-solution' model so much as it does to white water rafting where time-critical decisions have to be made to avoid obstacles and seize opportunities without the possibility of pausing. What many corporate computer users understand is that the key to identifying corporate threats and opportunities lies locked in the corporate data which is often embedded in legacy systems on obsolescent technologies. And they realise that the business needs to get at that data today.

Information technology is no longer restricted to automating back-office operations but is increasingly to be found on the desktops of senior executives and software competencies are increasingly to be found in the business area. Corporations have sound reasons to champion technology and a technology-literate management culture. Many corporations in the nineteen-eighties focus on acquisitions and takeovers as a means of growing the business. The nineties are going to be more about focusing on organic expansion by getting more out of the current customer base and optimising the opportunities presented by applying a more sophisticated and strategic policy towards current customers, current markets and current products. When it comes to examining new directions in information technology, many corporations have a problem distinguishing the really valuable applications from the background noise and constant hum of new software innovation. This problem can be exacerbated in a topic such as the data warehouse where the innovation is not centred primarily in the reasonably familiar arena of hardware and software, but in *architecture*. Failing to recognise the value of appropriate new innovations in the application of information technology is going to result in some corporations being 'blindsided' by failing to comprehend the strategic impact of such systems.

The centre of gravity in the structure and cultures of organisations is also shifting, especially in terms of an increased focus on the role of specialist knowledgeworkers at the expense of generalist management. This trend is accompanied by a steady movement away from command-and-control style of organisational cultures to the project-oriented modular corporation. One of the key attributes of the new organisational structure is the empowerment of first line managers in the enterprise, and access to information is a key ingredient in this process. Another key feature of the new culture is the creation of cross- functional teams which will quickly precipitate a demand for cross-functional information. These organisational trends will *drive* and *be driven by* new corporate information systems dedicated to the task to supporting strategic and operational decision making. In this respect there is a concerted effort throughout the industrialised world to move from being reactive and using control information to manage by exception, to a new vision-driven agenda for the enterprise.

Layers of management in the traditional hierarchical structure neither manage nor make decisions and their purpose as described by Peter Drucker is: 'to serve as "relays" : human boosters for the faint unfocused signals that pass for communications in the pre-information organisation.' [1]

Now some organisations are beginning to break the decision support log-jam by implementing corporate decision support systems which are increasingly conforming to the concept of the data warehouse. In very many instances the dynamic of the data warehouse is leading to fundamental changes in the design of the interface between the enterprise and the external market. This is tending to be driven by a policy of micro-segmentation of markets on the basis of data patterns which allows the enterprise to observe over time from the behaviour of data the corresponding behaviour patterns of their customers. Here is to be found the technological catalyst which will enable the industrial transformation of corporations from models of mass production to models of mass customisation of goods and services. Merely satisfying the customer is no longer acceptable; it is necessary to *delight* the customer. Keeping up with the competition is no longer a guarantee of survival; now it is necessary to *surprise* the competition. In a mass customised market, data pattern analysis will become an agent of revolution in the hands of creative people.

The core thesis being proposed here is based on four simple and direct premises. The first is that there is locked inside the sea of corporate data valuable patterns of information which are of key significance in guiding the business. The second is that this information will form the basis of unique services to customers in a manner that will transform the understanding which the enterprise may have of the market. The third is that the shortening of the distance between the identification of strategy and the execution of strategy will progressively transform the understanding which the enterprise may have of its own organisational structure. Because these individual assertions have been made previously and by renowned commentators then it must be assumed that there is general agreement and that the lack of progress in the implementation of such systems is explained by a less enthusiastic accord on the fourth premise: that the means of constructing such systems is available now. The absence of data warehouse 'solutions' on offer by the hardware and software vendors has meant that any enterprise undertaking the data warehouse project has had to manage the systems integration aspects of the project themselves. This has represented different degrees of difficulty for different enterprises and the degree of difficulty will depend on the level of 'disintegration' of the data in the first instance.

The corporate data warehouse may be defined in terms of six key characteristics which differentiate the data warehouse from other database systems in the enterprise.

The data in the data warehouse is:

(1)   *Separate* from the operational systems in the enterprise and populated by data from these systems.

(2)   *Available* entirely for the task of making data available to be interrogated by business users.

(3)   *Integrated* on the basis of a standard enterprise model.

(4)   *Time stamped* and associated with defined periods of time, i.e. calendar periods or fiscal reporting periods.

(5)   *Subject oriented,* most usually on the basis of 'Customer'.

(6)   *Non-volatile*, to the extent that updates do not occur on an individual basis.

(7)   *Accessible* to users who have a limited knowledge of computer systems or data structures.

(8)   *Non-volatile*, meaning that only batch updates are allowed to update the warehouse data.

The goal of the data warehouse is not only to satisfy the demands of the present -- for more accurate, integrated and timely *control* information -- but to transcend the internally focused control culture by using data patterns (derived from data sourced from inside and outside of the enterprise) to identify events which trigger *strategic* decisions which impact on the entire environment. Therefore the data warehouse is not just a software tool to do better what has been done before, but a management tool to do what has never been satisfactorily done before.

The data warehouse is, in essence, the engine which converts the churning mass of raw data into usable information which completely meets the demand for 'the right information in the right format at the right time'. But the real achievement of the data warehouse is that it re-defines the nature of information. The past era of computerisation will be characterised by systems which were applied to processes which in turn generated data. In the future era, many investments in information technology will be applied to data pattern analysis which in turn will spawn new processes.

Data warehousing is, essentially, a response to the problems and constraints that exist in corporate computing. it is an acknowledgement that we have failed to integrate operational applications. We have failed to adequately model the data or impose corporate data standards. we have not taken account of the reporting requirements of decision makers. we have not ensured that the data in corporate databases is clean and consistent. However depressing these failures are they do not, on their own, represent a charter for data warehousing. the primary driver of data warehousing is not the shortcomings of the past. Data warehousing is being driven by fundamental changes in the way business is conducted in the marketplace. These changes demand that transaction level customer data be captured and analysed. And no amount of tinkering around with the legacy systems is going to deliver that.

In the coming 'Age of Information', data will not just comprise entities in a database which have got attributes and relations but data will have *texture* through which hidden structures and patterns can be revealed. This will fundamentally transform our understanding of information from 'something we desire to know' to 'something which could never have otherwise been knowable'.

Chapter 2
_____ Information Enterprises:
The Early Innovators

Only a very few corporations have gone the route of 'information' and have made
the big investment in bringing together all of their corporate data in a data
warehouse type environment. They have tended, by and large, to have been US-
based Fortune 500 companies and they have tended, by and large, to be located in
highly competitive cauldrons. Because of the very nature of _data pattern analysis_
the outputs are regarded by these early innovators as highly confidential and so
too are the systems which are designed to produce the patterns.

In a widely acclaimed article Max D. Hopper, the senior vice-president for
information systems at American Airlines (where the exceptionally successful
SABRE yield management reservation system was developed) declared the
following :

> The role of information technology has always been to help organisations solve
> critical business problems or deliver new services by collecting data, turning data
> into information and turning information into knowledge quickly enough to reflect
> the time value of knowledge. For thirty years, much of our money and energy has
> focussed on the first stage of the process – building hardware, software, and
> networks powerful enough to generate useful data. That challenge is close to being
> solved; we have got our arms around the data gathering conundrum. The next stage,
> and the next arena for competitive differentiation, revolves around the
> intensification of analysis. Astute managers will shift their attention from
> _systems_ to _information_. [2]

Data warehousing is not so much an emerging technology as it is an emerging
architecture which makes possible the kinds of informating application which
were not previously feasible. So far, it has proliferated in three distinct industrial
sectors. These industries are (1) retailing, (2) banking, and (3)
telecommunications.

THE IMPETUS OF COMPETITION

The very early adopters in the USA seem to have been in retailing, commencing in the early to mid-1980s, followed by banking and telecommunications and later by airline companies. While it is not the purpose of the book to establish on a scientific basis data patterns which were previously undiscovered, the following general observations of these industries may be made. The breakup of AT&T in 1984 saw telecommunications in the USA enter a period of intense competitive activity. Banking and insurance became the subject of regulatory pressures which opened up the market in the same period. The airline industry has endured chronic deregulation and competition in the late eighties. And retailing was always a savage competitive pit. The common factor which triggers investment in data warehousing appears to be competitive intensity. While the sample is not yet sufficiently large or the research sufficiently comprehensive, this general correlation may be asserted. It can be asserted with even more confidence when one considers that the *first* two telecommunications companies in Europe to invest in data warehouse technology in the late eighties were Televerket in Sweden and British Telecom in the United Kingdom. These were the *first* two European countries to voluntarily deregulate their telecommunications markets and permit a second network operator to offer service. The deregulation frenzy being planned for the single European market is going to see the investment in pattern analysis engines grow dramatically.

One disturbing aspect to this putative pattern is that data warehousing did not appear to be a voluntary initiative but is precipitated only by dramatic external events. This would imply that the impetus to invest in a data warehouse solution must be more than moderate − it must be compelling!

In a 1993 survey of United States and European industry, compiled by Database Associates International, regarding attitudes to the concept of the data warehouse by corporations which had begun to examine this subject, the vast majority cited competitive advantage as the main benefit which they expected to accrue from the deployment of a data warehouse. It should be noted that the survey was directed only at large corporate enterprises which might reasonably be expected to have large volumes of unintegrated data. It is, nonetheless, consistent with the initial take-up pattern for any new product or concept which commences with implementations by early adopters who are of sufficient size to absorb the risk and uncertainty, and following a successful initial phase, the product/concept then experiences a rapid penetration of the market.

Two significant themes are clearly demonstrated by the Database Associates survey. The first is that the integration of data was cited by the largest number of respondents as the main reason why the data warehouse was being deployed. The second theme was that the largest number of respondents cited sales and marketing applications as the reason integrated data sets were so urgently required by the enterprise.

THE RETAILING INDUSTRY

Consumer club cards are increasingly being offered to customers by major chains of retailers. The principle is simple. The customer receives a card which he/she presents each time a purchase is made. This identifies the customer and is the key link between a raw mass of data and the means to derive commercially useful patterns. By using the card customers accumulate points which enable them to receive gifts, avail themselves of discounts etc. Part of the purpose of the consumer club is to reward customer loyalty and to encourage callbacks. But the more radical business benefit lies in the data that is being captured in the process. The retailer can now tell what customers are buying what products. For most retailers this critical link between sales and customer was always missing. All persons who entered a retail outlet were all equally anonymous — they were simply customers. Sales trends would indicate that some products were selling better than others and that some regions had different requirements than others. But why some customers purchased a toothbrush and some a fitted kitchen was just one of those unfathomable mysteries. The important pieces of market intelligence were generally only to be found in the folklore of the shop. For example, warehouse staff might complain about peculiar trends in stock throughput, or checkout staff might observe that customers who purchased one product generally bought another product after a few weeks had elapsed. But nothing generally happens as a result of this canteen conversation because no correlation can be established without analysing data at a detailed level. The breakthrough comes when the individual buying pattern of identifiable customers is observed and compared against models of cyclical and seasonal norms which might be expected to be present. At this stage customised marketing can transform the business. The consumer club is more important as a means of making this link than as a straightforward customer incentive scheme.

Case History 1. Ertl Toys is a 2,000 person company that makes childrens toys. they know that a product is only a hit as long as it holds the young consumers attention. For Ertl the problem was to be able to respond to this fickle demand quickly. The data warehouse uses market data to trigger the manufacturing process and the warehouse supports ad hoc queries as well as sales and marketing applications. This kind of data warehouse project is common in the retailing industry where companies are attempting to be genuinely market-led rather than production-driven.

Case History 2. In December 1989 K-Mart, one of the largest retail chains in the USA, had a problem. A Christmas doll called 'Holiday Moments' was failing to move off the shelves and it seemed that the giant retailer was going to be stuck with 36 000 of the $29.97 dolls. However, the information systems moved to the rescue as a data warehouse type system guided managers through a carefully calculated series of daily markdowns so that by Christmas Day all but a few dolls were sold – and none at a discount greater than 25%. At the same time the computer had spotted that a $1.97 plastic ornament was selling heavily which quickly triggered a re-order event. In these two simple instances in the space of a few short weeks K-Mart estimated the increase to their bottom line to be $250 000.

Human beings can spot a lot of these patterns after the event; but by then it is too late. Carefully modelled information applications trawling through detailed data in a data warehouse environment can identify the emerging pattern while the pattern is still at the formation stage. This enables the enterprise to react in time. It is real-time decision making.

Case History 3. Wal-Mart, another chain of US retailers has implemented a logistical support system which is virtually unequalled in the retailing industry. The system enables goods which are in transit to move from one loading dock to another without ever entering inventory. This technique of 'cross-docking' is driven by point-of-sale information being screened, analysed and transmitted via private satellite to Wal-Mart's suppliers. In this way decisions are not being made by managers deciding what products to 'push' into what stores – instead the customers through their purchasing behaviour are deciding what products to 'pull' into various outlets in the retail network. This is an impressive and dramatic example of an enterprise which understands the value of *data* as well as the critical importance of *time*.

Case History 4. VF Corporation is one of the world's largest publicly held clothing companies in the world. They face the challenge of providing what is required by the consumer in a volatile market where styles can change, in the process dating large quantities of stock which are still in inventory. The company responded to this challenge by constructing a state-of-the-art Market Response System (MRS) which is a customer-driven system populated with data from points of sale in retail outlets. The complexity of the task being faced by VF can be gauged by the fact that they have 300 retail partners and manage inventory on 9 500 styles at 27 000 stores. The system is used to improve market responsiveness and to ensure that flow replenishment is determined by a comprehensive knowledge of up-to-the-minute customer trends.

With the MRS system the 125-day product development cycle has been reduced to just 35 days, which allows manufacturers and retailers to change designs within the same selling season. Perhaps the biggest breakthrough in complex pattern analysis has occurred in this area of retail stock monitoring. The objective is to match the demand for particular goods in particular stores with a supply of that product – perhaps re-directing it from stores where that product is moving slowly. The benefits in the management of working capital – the life blood of retailing – are obviously enormous.

The high-level goal set for the MRS system was called 40-30-20. This represented a 40% reduction in cycle time, a 30% reduction in inventory and a 20% reduction in costs. These are ambitious targets and VF are confident that they will be achieved. It is significant that the VF example, like other data warehouse implementations, incorporates the concept of a business partnership – in this case between the manufacturing enterprise and the retailing enterprises.

THE BANKING AND INSURANCE INDUSTRIES

'Know your customer' is an old adage of sales but increasingly many corporations do not know their own customers. In an ironical way, the computer has been to blame for this situation. Historically, a bank had an intimate knowledge of its customers because there was a recognisable human interface between the customer and the enterprise. However, with the advent of computerised systems, automated teller machines and automated bank processes, the customer became remote and anonymous. The customer's employer lodges his/her salary directly into a bank account and the customer makes withdrawals from an ATM machine and receives statements and chequebooks in the post. It is convenient, but is also grossly alienating. The customer only visits the bank now every few years when they need a mortgage or loan and their eligibility for this service will be determined more on the basis of some commonly applied formula than on the actual behaviour of that customer. It is not uncommon for a customer who has maintained their account in credit for many years to receive a series of threatening letters simply because they took an extended holiday abroad and were unable to manage routine lodgements and their account became overdrawn by a trivial amount. It is infuriating, but it happens all the time. Similarly, a business customer may be a large and important customer of a bank and yet find that their credit card is cancelled by a bank official who is blissfully unaware that the customer has several other accounts in credit and is held in high esteem by another department of the bank. This is extremely dangerous, but it also happens all the time. Ultimately it is not the bad public relations which damages the enterprise as much as the bad decisions which are made and which could easily be averted by using a resource which the enterprise owns – its data.

Insurance companies deal with risk and risk can be identified through careful observation of variables which can act to increase the level of risk which can obtain at any given time. The insurance business itself is experiencing rapid change driven by a combination of factors, including an increasingly sophisticated consumer base, increased competition, and a proliferation in the combinations and variations in the financial products which are being offered. Pattern analysis is the identification of correlations at a more deeply embedded level than trend analysis. A trend is normally identified through the *behaviour* of data which may be extrapolated to identify a forecast. For example, an increase in insurance claims from young motorcyclists during the winter months may be observed as a trend with two variables. A pattern is more concerned with the *shape* of the data or the identification of a hidden structure in a massive pool of data. For example, recurring insurance claims from motorcyclists in a particular region, all of whom have a similar occupation, may be observed as a pattern. A pattern is not usually as discernible or as clear as a trend and only very rarely will a pattern come to light from human observation.

Case History 5. Citicorp, one of the largest US retail banks implemented a data warehouse type system in the late 1980s. In the early implementation of the system, two mainframe computers processing operational applications channelled their data on to a database computer utilised for market research. Prior to the implementation of the data warehouse the data required for market research tended to be months old before it was available in a usable form. The market research database system, dubbed BRIMS for Banking Relationship Information Management System, handles 1 500 requests annually for complex queries, many of which impact strategically on the direction of the enterprise.

Among the BRIMS components is a catalogue of banking relationships divided into households, not just individual customer accounts. For instance, a bank official can see data on all of the cheque and savings accounts, mortgages, certificates of deposit and other Citibank products and services which a family utilises. Such information enables the bank to identify gaps in the services being used or the opportunity to offer or to customise a suite of services to meet the needs that can be identified.

BRIMS also includes an account management facility which analyses household information from a revenue perspective and this enables the bank to identify their most valuable customers. The system also enables the bank to simulate the impact of policy changes which may be employed to convert less profitable customers into higher margin ones. And finally, there are the ad hoc queries – the powerful essence of the data warehouse. Instead of mailing blindly to thousands of customers in New York, the individual banker who is marketing home equity loans can navigate through the integrated data and enquire 'the names of households that have taken out mortgages in the last five years, do not already have home equity loans and live on Long Island'. The deliverable from the system can be a list of customised letters.

The difference in sales between 'cold-calling' and 'hot pursuit' is immense. And more to the point, only Citicorp has that data, just as any other enterprise has the sole advantage of owning data about its customer base. The competitor only gets that data after the customer has been won away.

THE TELECOMMUNICATIONS INDUSTRY

Telecommunications companies have been to the fore in the race to build the most advanced data warehouses. Why telecommunications companies and not other utilities is probably explained by the theory that competitive intensity is the main driver of data pattern analysis initiatives and the deregulation of telecommunications in the USA and now in Europe is well established as political policy. The standard unit of telecommunications usage in voice telephony is based on 'pulses' or 'toll tickets' which is normally a measure of a unit of time consumed by the telephone customer. Traditionally, telephone companies had a use for this data only to bill customers. When the customer had paid the bill then there was no more use for the data.

But telephone companies, like most utilities, suffer from two fundamental problems. The first is that the network must be designed and configured to handle the *peaks* of traffic that occur during the day. For the greater part of the day the network is only being using at a fraction of its capacity and this has severe implications for the efficiency of the capital investment. The second problem faced by utilities is the problem of differentiating a commodity service. After all, one person making a telephone call for three minutes is pretty much like any other person making a three-minute call. In this environment there are no obvious ways of stimulating demand.

Through the implementation of a data warehouse the two problems effectively solve each other. The objective is to segment customers so that they can be differentiated on the basis of behaviour. This behaviour will be identified from the usage patterns that are exhibited by the customer. Then different customers in different segments are offered discounts based on customised 'call plans'. Customers will only be able to avail themselves of the discount if they make specific categories of call during specified time bands. The net effect is to stimulate traffic, since the customer is receiving a cheaper service, and to 'even out' the peaks and troughs in the pattern of traffic on the network.

Case History 6. US West is one of the Baby Bell operating companies (Regional Bell Operating Companies) and it has over 12 million customers located in the 'mountain states'. At the time of the company formation in 1984 US West was a conglomeration of a number of separate regional Bell organisations, each of which had its own separate information systems. Therefore there was an urgent need to integrate the data (especially the customer and account data) from the diverse systems in order to provide a 'picture' of the entire customer base. What US West constructed was a Corporate Subject Data Base (CSDB) which integrated all of the services used by an account. Then a sophisticated segmentation model was introduced which enables the company to customise the products, services and discount deals which could be offered to customers. In addition, the data patterns can provide an indication of the areas where investments in the network should be targeted. US West adopted a useful and sensible approach to the data warehouse which they referred to as 'incremental tactical deployment'. What this meant was that a number of prioritised areas were selected and the each area was implemented on the warehouse in incremental steps.

The ability of US West to segment its customer base down to fine levels of granularity and to reconstitute these segments in response to a very competitive position is a dramatic indication of how enterprises in the future are going to use strategic data to respond with alacrity to complex changes in the external environment.

CONCLUSION

The common denominators which can observed from the kinds of enterprise and the kinds of data warehouse implementation which these enterprises tend to deploy fall into three categories. Firstly, there is the common denominator of competitive pressure. Secondly there is the common denominator of mass market producers experiencing the transition to a more customised system of production. Finally there is the common denominator of the data warehouse system being driven by the need to significantly alter internal processes in the enterprise.

Chapter 3
The Case For Utilising Corporate Data: the Basis for Strategic Advantage

STRATEGIC AND OPERATIONAL DECISION MAKING

When analysing the requirements for data in an enterprise it will be necessary to define these requirements in terms of *strategic* requirements and *operational* requirements. The characteristics of these two kinds of information need are distinctly different and are set out in Table 3.1. As a general rule of thumb it may be asserted that a data warehouse may be designed to accommodate both the operational and the strategic view of the data, or may be justified on the basis of the strategic requirements only. In instances where the requirements for data to support decision making are purely operational then it may be worth considering if this requirement can be met by investing in the existing operational transaction systems.

One important issue which it is worth drawing attention to in respect of the properties compared in the table is the matter of granularity (i.e. the level of detail of the data). Traditionally it may have been assumed that strategic decision makers had a requirement for summarised and aggregated data only and that operational decision makers had a requirement for detailed data only. In the opinion of this author that is a seriously flawed perspective. The importance of having detailed data for the strategic user is to afford them the opportunity to derive individual data patterns from the detailed data. High-level views of data can certainly provide evidence of trends but detailed data is necessary to discern patterns in behaviour of customers, employees, suppliers etc. The distinction between strategic and operational decision support systems are outlined in Table 3.1.

Table 3.1

	Data	Strategic	Operational
	Accuracy	General accuracy	Absolute accuracy
	Boundary	Integrated	Functional
	Coverage	Long (historical data)	Short (real-time data)
	Timeliness	Days/Weeks	Urgent/immediate
	Granularity	Aggregate & detailed	Detailed only
	Secondary query	Normal	Rare
	Query definition	Ad hoc/Once-off	Repeatable

THE CHANGING CHARACTERISTICS OF DECISION MAKING

The general characteristics of decisions being made in commercial and administrative environments are undergoing substantial change at present, with increasing pressure being brought to bear on the decision makers to take a more holistic perspective on the impact of the decision. The changes which are being experienced are set out in Table 3.2

Table 3.2

Decision Relation	Past Characteristic	Future Characteristic
Response	Scheduled	Urgent
Maker	Generalist	Specialist
Focus	Internal	External
Risk	Moderate	High
Objective	Control	Strategy
Environment	Stable	Turbulent
Boundary	Functional	Corporate
Technology	Transactional	Interactive
Basis	Item	Pattern
Change	Incremental	Fundamental
Orientation	Present	Future
Enabler	Organisation	Technology

The Communication Gap And Information Overload

The 'communication gap' has long been a staple standby of every management consultancy exercise. Which is not necessarily to belittle the necessary endeavours of management consultants since the 'communication gap' was a manifest reality throughout the industrialised world. Most corporations have responded to this apparent deficiency by making a fetish of communication. Now every piece of data concerning every process and event is circulated to every business manager who in turn circulates it to their staff. Some of the data is useful, a lot is irrelevant and harmless and a good deal is positively distracting and/or misleading. What exists is not so much a 'communications gap' as a 'clarity gap'.

What is required to overcome the 'clarity gap' is a threefold initiative. Firstly, the key information needs of each corporate decision maker should be radically simplified and expressed in relation to the business goals which they are seeking to achieve (this stage should not be interpreted as rigidly specifying their information needs, which is quite a different thing). Secondly, the key information needs of different decision makers should be integrated so that they are congruent with each other. And finally, the decision makers should have access to the same data sets via an interface that the user can employ to access the data when the decision maker decides to do so. All other information which does not directly support the business process engaged on by the decision maker belongs in a physical or electronic noticeboard, or in the company magazine.

THE CORPORATE DATA RESOURCE

The strategic importance of information relates to its use in formulating business decisions. And business decisions occur in a variety of ways. It may be that the data is required as a catalyst for creative thinking, or for accurate analysis, or in acquiring or allocating resources, or in assessing the impact of events, or in evaluating alternative actions, or in establishing general principles. In all of these common decision making situations complete data relating to the action under consideration is essential. This information needs to reflect even the most dynamic of processes and the most fluid of situations in order to comprehensively remodel the posture of the enterprise in response to unpredictable internal and external events. In this way the enterprise can function in a manner which is most advantageous to the supply and demand conditions of the marketplace and, most importantly, can do so before their competitors.

When we speak of companies which are 'flexible,' what is normally meant is that they are responsive to the consumer demands of the market. The means by which an enterprise can become 'flexible' is twofold. It must have flexible processes embodied in operational information systems which allow the enterprise to respond to consumer behaviour. But first it must have decision support systems which can identify what that behaviour is. A great many organisations have devoted a great deal of investment to ensuring that their business processes function flexibly as the enterprise is buffeted by market forces. These systems may be very impressive in their ability to flexibly adapt to new products and services, or to new discounts, or to an integrated pricing package, or to a new marketing policy. But these operational systems are still *reacting* to events. What has attracted a good deal less investment in the past are systems designed to guide the decision maker towards *which* policy to pursue.

The systems which automate the activities of the enterprise and the systems which support decision making in the enterprise are symbiotically linked, but in the future will not be the same systems. And to have one without the other is to fail to maximise the existing investment which has been made. To have both growing in concert with each other is to have a formidable platform for competitive advantage in the business environment of the next decade. Each of the two computing environments will act as an agent of re-engineering on the other.

DECISION THEORY

Decision Theory
Decision theory is a way of approaching a decision in a logical systematic and structured fashion in order to arrive at an optimum solution. Normally an optimum solution is the 'best course of action' which may be taken where a number of alternative courses of action are available. Different structured techniques may be employed in order to indicate the 'best course of action'. The most common structured techniques used for this purpose are the following :

(1) Decision trees, which comprise a graphical representation of a tree with many 'decision branches' leading to certain 'outcomes' radiating from a 'decision node'.When probabilities are assigned to an outcome, then an optimum decision is identified.
(2) Payoff tables, which estimates the payoff in respect of each alternative decision and outcome.
(3) Risk and utility analysis, which allows for more caution than simply determining the payoff. The utility of the decision is the balance of probability between the payoff and the risk associated with a given outcome.

Of course, all of these techniques are open to the charge of being too simplistic or too rudimentary a framework to support complex decisions occurring in a fluid and dynamic environment. Such techniques are also based on some element of prejudice, since the probabilities may have to be assigned without the assistance of a decision support system.

However, what is clear is that the determination of quality decisions and the estimation of outcomes and risks should only be based on valid information. Any contrary view which proposes the supremacy of executive intuition along with the occasional bit of industrial espionage betrays a regression back to a time when important decisions were based on the studious examination of animal entrails.

The likelihood of decision support systems 'making' strategic decisions is still a long way off, but the stage at which such systems can make operational decisions is already here and the stage at which information systems can 'assist' in making strategic decisions is also upon us. It is more likely in the short term that key decisions will be made on the basis of extensive SWOT (Strengths, Weaknesses, Threats, and Opportunities) analysis and will still require a good deal of judgement. But increasingly, the judgements will be made on the basis of available information and, over time, the proportion of judgements which need to be made will diminish.

Cognitive Psychology and the Decision Making Process
Research in the field of cognitive psychology has demonstrated that a majority of decision makers in a variety of situations are strongly influenced by prejudice. It is not generally a conscious prejudice. It has been amply demonstrated through research in the field of cognotive psycology [3] that, when determining the probability of future events, decision makers are guided by data which is heavily biased because it is the most easily available data to apply to the decision, or it is the data that occurs most frequently and so is embedded in the short-term memory of the decision maker, or it is data that is recent and therefore still lodged in the short-term memory. In the lexicon of psychology this tendency is explained by the 'availability heuristic' (decisions guided by data which is readily available, though quite likely to be incomplete) and the 'representative heuristic' (decisions guided by data based on familiar representational models, which are quite likely to be inappropriate). In each of these two tendencies the decision making process is, in essence, intuitive. Of course, the existence of a corporate store of integrated data will not alter established norms of cognitive behaviour in decision makers which will still be substantially based on heuristics, but the canvas of availability will be considerably enlarged.

Modes of Thinking
Edward de Bono [4], one of the most widely read cognitive psychologists, argues that the attention of an individual can only be directed at one specific part of the 'memory-surface', i.e. only a small part of the large pattern is retained; the rest is ignored. In this model the process of exploring, analysing and learning is facilitated by combining separate patterns into a single unified pattern. The

cognitive process by which data is selected, segregated and combined is still too poorly understood by software engineers for a really significant advance to be made in the field of decision support applications but it represents one of the most promising areas of research in computer science. de Bono's categorisation of the thinking process provides a useful initial model by which the impact of decision support systems may be understood. In this model there are four categories of thinking – natural thinking, logical thinking, mathematical thinking, and lateral thinking.

Natural thinking is a crude and primitive response to information which proceeds to a decision on the basis of the prominence of the information or through the repetition of information. Generally speaking, natural thinking is a dubious basis for decision making. Yet, in some enterprises key decisions are still based on poorly justified 'facts' which are meekly accepted by the body corporate. These 'facts' may have resulted from a survey conducted long ago, or from the strongly held conviction of some senior executive, or from some incomplete information, or from information compiled for a purpose different from the one which has given rise to the 'fact'. And so, for whatever reason, the corporate myth endures that 'product X' is the most profitable product among the range of products being produced by the enterprise.

Logical thinking occurs in a more rational and controlled fashion where the unproven assumptions of natural thinking are factored out. Logical thinking eliminates the excesses of natural thinking but also curbs the possibilities of creative thinking. Existing computerised control systems, however fragmented and inadequate, provide a basis for a logical process of thinking and decision making. Therefore, in a logical mode of thinking the costs and revenues of all products can be compared and the most profitable product identified. This is rational behaviour but it can also be sterile and limiting.

Mathematical thinking is based on devising a formula or algorithm which is used to process data. For example, the cost and revenue data associated with a range of products can be presented simply as 'profit by product expressed in money' or 'product profit expressed as a percentage of total profit' or any other number of variables. Mathematical thinking is used extensively in existing decision support systems as a means of presenting data in 'canned' reports. However, the initial selection of data limits the scope of mathematical thinking since there are only so many ways that the same data can be usefully packaged and presented.

Lateral Thinking is the fourth category identified by de Bono and is concerned with rearranging the data that is available so that the familiar established pattern of the data is transformed into a new and different pattern. He observed, 'with other kinds of thinking you know what you are looking for. With lateral thinking you may not know what you are looking for until you find it'. Lateral thinking is an attempt not to engage in the selection process which inhibits the other modes of thinking and seeks to explore all options, even those which do not appear to be logical, and to re-examine all fixed assumptions. Lateral thinking complements conventional (vertical) thinking and is an important means of discovering new strategic opportunities. For example, the lateral thinker may decide that product profitability is not an appropriate means of measuring product potential and may discover by exploring different patterns that certain customer segments always buy product A after another segment in the same region buys Product B. Now this is a truly useful and interesting piece of information.

In later work [5] de Bono differentiates between proactive thinking and reactive thinking. In reactive thinking all of the facts (data) are available and the decision maker assembles the facts to form a pattern which identifies the optimum solution. In pro-active thinking not all of the facts are available.

Socio-cultural Norms of Decision Making

Because the historical pattern of corporate decision making has evolved in a world of incomplete information, it is the case that most organisational cultures do not exalt an exclusively 'rational' or 'scientific' mode of decision making. This is probably just as well since a reliance on exclusively empirical evidence to determine strategy would have been hopelessly naive, given the crude level of decision support offered by decision support information systems in the past.

Now, however, the deployment of data warehouse solutions signals the beginning of the end of the political-intuitive modes of decision making. In the field of organisational science Chin and Benne [6] draw attention to the attachment which people have for the behavioural norms in which they have been immersed. They observe:

> Patterns of action and practice are supported by socio-cultural norms and by commitments on the part of individuals to these norms. Changes in normative orientation involve changes in attitudes, values, skills, and significant relationships, not just changes in knowledge information, or intellectual rationales for action and practice. [7]

It should be clear, therefore, that the data warehouse cannot be driven by the information technology department in isolation from the wider business. The project may become, for many enterprises, as much of an organisational intervention as an information systems initiative. Failure to take account of the socio-cultural agenda in the course of the data warehouse project will result in the deployment of a resplendent technological white elephant.

'Dissonance' in Decision Making

There is compelling evidence offered by social psychologists that decision making is often an arbitrary and inconsistent process. This occurs largely because of the existence of prejudice (conscious or unconscious) in the mind of the decision maker which leads him or her towards making a *natural* rather than a *rational* assessment of a situation. In this regard a theory of 'cognitive dissonance' was developed by Leon Festinger [8] to explain how an individual can hold two separate opinions or beliefs which are inconsistent or contradictory. For example, a corporate decision maker may decide that a particular discount promotion would result in a positive demand elasticity and therefore increase revenue. That same decision maker may also decide to curtail credit available to particular customer segments, including customers being targeted by the sales promotion. This situation may arise because the decision maker is responding rationally to two separate sets of data culled from separate sources and assembled selectively by separate constituencies. Unfortunately, the sum total of the two decisions is not rational. Very often organisations will demonstrate symptoms of dissonance as different parts of the organisation adopt policies which are odds with each other. And when the decision maker is emotionally and politically tied to the decision(s) which he or she has adopted the decision is more likely to become irrevocable in spite of any further empirical evidence which is offered to refute the correctness of the original decision. This tendency to rationalise the decision (i.e. to reduce the dissonance being experienced) with all available data which conveniently supports the original decision is a defensive reaction all too common in corporate life. Elliot Aronson observes of this behaviour:

> Dissonance reducing behaviour is irrational. By this I mean that it is often maladaptive, in that it can prevent people from learning important facts or from finding real solutions to their problems. [9]

The Pattern of Corporate Decision Making

The pattern of work of most senior executives does not generally conform to a pattern of data interrogation or even of information evaluation and analysis. Top management work in a fragmented fashion, forever in demand by the internal organisation and by the external environment. The essence of their role is political – it is their job to motivate, to co-ordinate, to inform, and to represent. And most of all, they need to influence and persuade. They need to persuade the customer, the employees, the corporate partners, the corporate lenders, the shareholders, the suppliers, the media and the government. These are not tasks which are amenable to computerisation, nor is it practicable to assert that top executives should stop doing these things in order to focus exclusively on strategy formulation. In this regard it will be necessary to recognise that the task of generating queries to run against the data in the data warehouse and the task of studying the patterns that emerge will be a role for specialised knowledgeworkers. These specialised strategists will, most probably, be at the disposal of senior executives and these senior executives may regularly intervene with queries of their own and most definitely will have to authorise any course of action which may result from analysing the data. The key distinction which has bedevilled many attempts to design strategic decision support systems is the assumption that top executives *devise* strategy when, in fact, the role of top executives is to *authorise* strategy.

Many decision support systems also confuse the requirements for strategic data with the requirements for operational data. The nature of strategic data is quite distinct from operational data, operational management and operational systems where the mission is to *execute* strategy. If there is confusion in the enterprise on the matter of who devises strategy, who authorises strategy and who executes strategy, then it will inevitably follow that there will be considerable fragmentation and dysfunction evident in the decision support systems which are constructed around this confusion.

ALIGNING THE SOFTWARE SYSTEM WITH DECISION MAKING CULTURE

There are three high-level approaches which may be adopted by the designer of corporate decision support systems.

Firstly, the software designer may assiduously construct the system on the basis of the existing model of decision making in the enterprise. If the model for decision making is coherent and appropriate to the business, then the system is likely to be very successful and will add considerably to the quality of business decisions. If the environment for decision making is dysfunctional, then the system will mirror that dysfunction and will probably lead to a period of automated chaos followed by 'decision paralysis'.

Secondly, the software designer may decide to ignore the existing model of decision making and construct the decision support system based on a generic model of decision making. Very often this will tend to make the system very artificial and there will be a very slow takeup by users. The designer may also be tempted to construct the system on the basis of elegant or convenient technical considerations. This is invariably a mistake since the system will not be embedded in the culture of the organisation.

Thirdly, the software designer may seek to first critically examine the decision making process before seeking a requirement specification. In this way the construction of the decision support system can be used as the catalyst for redesigning the decision making environment. This is obviously the optimum approach, but the problem with this option is that it requires the enterprise to devote a good deal of time to a politically sensitive topic and absorb a lot of pain in addressing the issues which will arise. Unfortunately, many organisations see the corporate decision support system as the solution to their problems and fail to recognise that there is no decision making structure to support.

In many corporations strategic decision making may occur in an informal manner with various research groups and committees feeding different higher-level committees. Just as business processes are fragmented and functionally bounded so too is the corporate decision making process. The task of constructing a corporate decision support system will obviously threaten that structure and it may be the case that there will be considerable opposition to what may be perceived as 'centralising' decision making through the use of information systems.

Part of the reason for this is that no information systems which comprehensively support strategic decision making have been traditionally available to them. EIS systems have been used by senior executives, but usually as control tools. They see a performance variance on the screen of their EIS system and they promptly dispatch a memorandum to the functional manager concerned. This kind of reactive control oriented behaviour is precisely what a culture of data pattern analysis is *not* about.

THE BUSINESS DRIVERS OF DECISION SUPPORT SYSTEMS

The purpose of implementing information systems of any kind is driven by one of five different motivations.

(1)   *Reduced costs* in the enterprise by replacing human labour with an automated environment by implementing systems which carry out all of the tedium of calculations and by reducing the amount of working capital tied up in a business through the implementation of systems such as materials requirement planning systems (MRP) or just-in-time delivery systems (JIT). In the earliest days of   computerisation that was probably considered to be the only valid motivation for investing in information technology. The systems tended to be exclusively transactional and the decision support capability was negligible.

(2)   *Increased control* in the business environment by measuring performance against objectives and improving decision making by providing a 'hard' information basis for the strengths, weaknesses, threats and opportunities which guide the selection of operational decision options. This is normally achieved by control checks which are built into transaction systems as well as pre-defined reports which are generated by these systems and typically provide the user with a week-ending survey of costs, or productivity or sales. This was the beginning of the demand for decision support facilities in operational systems.

(3)   *Improved planning* in the business environment by refining and integrating the corporate planning process and by basing all suppositions, assumptions and probabilities on a sound informational basis. The kind of systems which have been used to support planning would come into the category of 'decision support' and include executive information systems (EIS) as well as financial and business simulation models. This trend marked the movement of decision support systems away from highly structured and purely operational decision support into the realm of unstructured strategic decision support. However, these systems were confined to highly summarised data.

(4)   *Increased quality* which is embedded in the business processes through the cross-checking of data, the validation of inputs to systems, the faster speed of response, the elimination of human error. These systems would typically include computer-aided design systems (CAD) as well as most administrative and financial systems. Generally, this motivation in implementing information systems had very little to do with obtaining improved decision support capabilities but it is significant because, for the first time, intangible corporate considerations were being offered to justify information technology investment.

(5)   *Increased revenue* by identifying opportunities for new products and services, or offerings for newly discovered market segments, or pricing or discounting packages, or market stimulation initiatives. It has not been until quite recently that companies have based information technology investments on an assertion that the investment would directly increase the existing revenue streams. This goal of increasing revenue through strategic positioning can be addressed by some operational systems but, increasingly, this will be the domain of the data warehouse. It is the latest stage on the road of decision support systems in the longer-term quest for the cybernetic machine.

Transaction systems have for a long time been able to generate 'canned' reports which satisfy the need for control information which generally are measures of operational performance against budgets and targets. Transaction systems have been successful in reducing costs, improving quality and increasing control. Some existing models for decision support such as EIS systems and business and financial modelling which are populated only by small volumes of aggregate and summary data have been used with *some* success to support corporate planning.

SOURCES OF DATA

Generally speaking, there are only two high-level categories of data populated on to a data warehouse environment and these are defined by source – internal data and external data. Internal data is data belonging to the enterprise and generated by operational transaction systems and this data describes activities which are happening *inside* the enterprise.

External data is that data which may be obtained or purchased by the enterprise and is normally data which describes activities happening *outside* the enterprise. One of the key objectives of the data warehouse database design is to integrate the internal and external data in a meaningful fashion.

Internal Data

Internal data is generated by the operational transaction systems in the enterprise and these are capable of being identified as clusters of software applications in different business functions. A typical large corporation with a mature information systems environment will have between 30 and 40 significant transaction-based information systems, and these may be replicated in different regions of the enterprise. For the purposes of identifying the source of corporate data which will be extracted and populated on to the data warehouse the functional clusters of information systems in the enterprise may be divided into seven categories, as follows.

(1) Financial systems. General Ledger System, Accounts Payable System, Accounts Receivable System, Budget Control System, Treasury Management System, Cost Accounting System.

(2) Logistics systems. Materials Requirement Planning (MRP) System, Fleet Transport System, Purchasing System, Distribution Control System.

(3) Sales systems. Multiple Service Order Systems for different products and services.

(4) Production systems. Production Control System, Works Order Tracking System, Project Tracking System, Quality Control System, Computer Integrated Manufacturing (CIM) Systems.

(5) Personnel systems. Personnel Records System, Payroll System, Staff Development & Training System.

(6) Billing systems. Multiple Billing Systems for different products and services.

(7) Information systems. Office Automation Systems, Electronic Bulletin Boards, Executive Information System, existing Decision Support Tools.

External Data

External data is captured outside of the enterprise and is, most often, made available at a cost by specialist information providers. Because the external environment *is* the difference between operational and strategic decision making, utilising data which describes the external environment is of critical importance. The purpose of analysing external data is threefold :

- To recognise opportunities
- To detect threats
- To identify synergies

The different kinds of external data will be clustered around the following categories :

(1) *Competitor data.* Products; services; pricing; sales promotions; mergers and takeovers.
(2) *Economic data.* Currency fluctuations; political indicators; interest rate movements; stock and bond prices.
(3) *Industry data.* Technology trends; marketing trends; management science and trade information.
(4) *Credit data.* Individual credit ratings and business viability assessments.
(5) *Commodity data.* Raw material prices.
(6) *Econometric data.* Income groups and consumer behaviour.
(7) *Psychometric data.* Consumer profiling.
(8) *Meterological data.* Weather conditions, rainfall, temperature.
(9) *Demographic data.* Age profiles; population densities.
(10) *Sales & marketing data.* Lists of prospective customers.

A good deal of the external data belongs in the electronic bulletin board type systems or else is available from the information supplier on a dial-up basis. This data is not likely to be integrated with the internal corporate data. On the other hand, key data elements which can add considerable value to the internal data would be candidates for integration. The econometric, psychometric and demographic data would be the most likely categories of external data that the enterprise would seek to integrate with the internal customer data. But this generalisation would not hold true for enterprises where key decisions are associated with specialised requirements. For example, the co-relation between manning levels (internal data) and weather forecasts (external data) might be a specific requirement in agriculture or in the transport industry. This would allow the enterprise to see its customers from another perspective and to deduce patterns which are valuable for the business which would not have been discernible from the internal data alone.

The most obviously valuable internal source of data is going to be the corporate billing systems which can identify some information about the customer including the essential information concerning the revenue generated by individual customers.

A key decision which an enterprise must make about the design of the data warehouse is the degree to which the decisions require detailed data and the degree to which summary data would suffice. For example, if customer data is being used for a mass marketing exercise, then aggregate data would normally suffice. If, however, the objective was to identify specific sales leads, then detailed data would be required. Here the designer is presented with three options.

(1) Detailed data.
(2) Aggregate data.
(3) Aggregate data and sampled detailed data.

The third option, sampled detailed data, is often something of a cost compromise since the implication is that detailed data is necessary but that the holding of detailed data in respect of all records is not justified by the value of the decision. Of course, none of these three options excludes an approach combing all three options. For example, the data warehouse might contain (a) detailed data on all customer accounts in a particular region for an intensive sales campaign there, (b) aggregate data on accounts nationally to support advertising and marketing strategy and (c) a random sample of detailed data on a specific market segment to monitor a new product recently launched at that segment.

When approaching data from a statistical perspective a number of techniques need to be employed in order to (a) analyse the data and (b) present the data. These techniques are outlined here in a superficial manner with a view only to introducing the reader to the richness of statistical techniques available. Statistical analysis is a specialism performed by trained personnel and one of the key risks which must be managed by enterprises intending to make large volumes of data available for analysis is the degree to which the analysts are equipped to come to terms with the data.

ANALYSIS TECHNIQUES

The purpose of providing all of the integrated corporate data to users is to enable the data to be analysed and this cannot be done long-term on the basis of ad hoc analysis. In order to construct applications which the user can use and re-use the designer of the applications will have to construct business models. After all, to have all of the data integrated in the one place is one thing. To do anything useful with the data is quite another. It would be a mistake of enormous proportions to expect that, just because business users have complained for decades that they do not have access to data, that they will necessarily know what to do with it.

In the early roll out of the data warehouse it will be necessary to build applications which interact in a structured manner with the sea of data in order to anchor the data warehouse to some applications which will deliver tangible early benefits to the business. In this way the user has a means of interrogating the data without having a detailed knowledge of the data or without having any particularly insightful query. In the beginning the objective will be to engage the user. And in the absence of clearly defined applications this will be done most easily by providing applications which perform fairly elementary statistical analysis of the data. Statistical techniques are generally divided into two categories. *Descriptive* statistics are used to describe the data and include diagrams, charts, tables and graphs. *Analytical* statistics seek to draw conclusions from the data which will guide the decision maker to the correct decision. These statistical applications may incorporate any number of the following common statistical analysis techniques.

Probability Analysis
Very often statistical analysis is concerned with establishing the probability of a given event. Probability is a forecast of a given event or condition which is measured on a scale from 0 to 1 where 0.5 represents a 50:50 probability of the event occurring. In determining the probability distribution, a calculation must be made of the frequency of what is known as the 'random variable' – that element which is subject to apparently random change. Data histories provide a basis for establishing the historic occurrences of the event being analysed.

Statistical Inference
Statistical inference may be used to draw conclusions from a sample about a larger population. Statistical inference is used extensively in market research, political polls, quality assurance testing and consumer reaction testing.

Hypothesis Testing
Hypothesis testing involves an assumption about what is referred to as a 'null hypothesis' which is the expected value and then to have an 'alternative hypothesis' which covers all other values. This technique is regularly used in quality control where the 'null hypothesis' is a value within the acceptable range of tolerances so that everything belonging to the 'alternative hypothesis' is, by definition, a reject.

Regression Analysis
Regression analysis is a technique which allows the analyst to identify the relationship between two variables. One variable (referred to as the 'dependent variable'), might be volume of sales. The other variables, referred to as the 'independent variables'), might be volume of expenditure on advertising, quality, information systems, distribution, or research. The object is to identify which independent variable has the most impact on the dependent variable.

Correlation Analysis
Like regression analysis, correlation analysis is concerned with establishing the relationship between two variables. Unlike regression analysis which *describes*

the relationship, correlation analysis is concerned with establishing the *extent* of the relationship. A value from +1 (two variables perfectly related in a positive sense, i.e. when one increases, the other increases) to -1 (two variables perfectly related in a negative sense, i.e. when one increases, the other decreases). Where the value is 0, there is no relationship.

It is necessary to express a word of caution about regression and correlation analysis since the existence of a relationship between two variables does not necessarily denote causality. The objective is to discover *meaningful* relationships between activities.

Composition Analysis
Composition analysis is concerned with identifying the makeup of different objects which can be analysed with a view to identifying changes in the composition of the object under analysis. For example, changes in the composition of markets, market segments, and market share are of intense interest to sales and marketing decision makers, while the composition of costs in an enterprise is generally the subject of intense analysis and may be the subject of a dedicated application specified by a cost or management accountant.

Value Added Analysis
Value added analysis is a useful technique for determining how much value is added to a product during different stages in the lifecycle of the product. Very often, it is the initial analysis which is carried out by business process re-engineering analysts, since the objective is to identify the processes (or components of processes) which do not add real value or are duplicated, redundant or dysfunctional.

Time Series Analysis
An observation of data over time yields useful analysis potential since it is essentially an observation of the behaviour of the data over time. This observation may identify one or more of the following phenomena.
(1)   A *Trend* may be exhibited by the behaviour of data over time and is
       normally plotted on an *x/y* graph. In the example presented in Figure 2 the
       sales volumes for three products (A, B, and C) are plotted. In this example
       there is evidence of a decrease in the sales volumes of products A and B
       concurrent with an upsurge in demand for product C. In this simple
       example there is clear evidence of product substitution occurring.

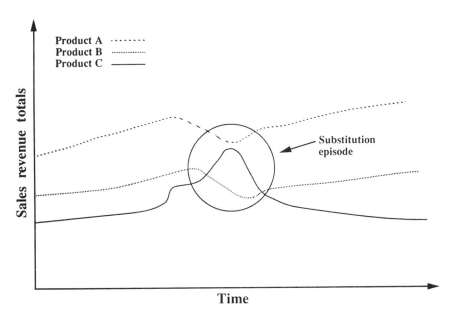

Figure 2 - 'Shape' in data (trend overlays)

(2) A *Cyclical Variation* may be exhibited by the behaviour of the data and
     this may be related to external events such as the performance of the
     economy. Cyclical variations will have a relationship to time that is not
     precise. This may be represented by a succession of waves plotted on a
     two-dimensional graph.

(3) A *Seasonal Variations* may be exhibited by a repeating pattern occurring in
     the data which is indicative of a precise relationship with time. For
     example, seasonal variations may be identified in the purchase of specific
     sporting equipment or the purchase of sun lotion, or the density of urban
     traffic over twenty-four hours.

(4) *A Pattern* may be exhibited through the observation of the 'shape' of the
     data and this may be plotted using a scattergraph as in Figure 3. In this
     example the sales volumes of a product (the dependent variable) are
     plotted against the expenditure on the promotion of the product (the
     independent variable). The 'shape' of the data implies a plateau tendency in
     the data such that any expenditure over a given level has no further
     appreciable impact on sales volumes.

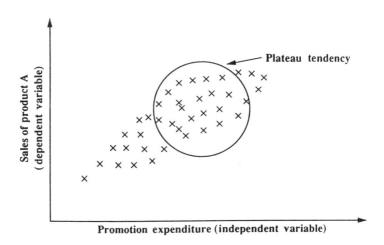

Figure 3 - 'Shape' in data (scattergraph)

Indices
Indices are normally used as a measure of performance in a control oriented system. These may be incorporated into a decision support system as a useful statistical shorthand to describe the performance of a particular activity. An index number will be determined for a base year from which the progressive performance is then measured according to a formula which is understood by the decision makers using the indices.

'What if' Analysis
From a business point of view, one of the most valuable functions which a decision support system can provide is the capacity to perform accurate 'What if' analysis against up-to-date production data. This, in many ways, is the essence of the business decision risk. There are multiple courses of action. Not all of them are right. Not all of them are wrong. But all of them have *consequences*.

Sensitivity Analysis
Sensitivity analysis is an analysis technique used to demonstrate the effects of slight or incremental changes to key objects in the business represented in the application model. The profitability of an activity may be based on a number of critical assumptions and could be dramatically altered by events which undermine these assumptions. For example, an otherwise profitable activity may be rendered very unprofitable by slight changes in the cost of raw materials or by currency fluctuations.

Impact Analysis

Very often in business, particularly in a functionally bounded enterprise, one of the most poorly perfected arts is to be able to assess the multiple impacts that a particular course of action in one part of the enterprise will have on other parts of the enterprise. For example, a change in pricing policy will have dramatic impacts on volume of sales, procurement of stores, the labour requirement, the return on capital employed on equipment, the migration of customers to other products, the migration of customers to competitors. And these are just a few. Each of these impacts will, in turn, trigger other impacts.

Proportion Disparity Analysis

This is the 80:20 rule familiar to everyone in business where the disparity of proportions has long been observed as a common phenomenon. For example, it is commonly asserted that 20% of the population own 80% of the wealth, or that 20% of the stock items in a stores represents 80% of the value of all stock, or that 20% of customers generate 80% of revenue in the enterprise. Sometimes referred as *Pareto analysis* and often represented on a *Lorenz curve* the discovery of proportion disparity in various activities in the business generally precipitates dramatic strategic re-alignments in the enterprise.

Chapter 4
The History of Decision Support Systems: a Record of Failure

When an information system is being designed there is a requirement for information at two levels. One has to do with the process (and the process will determine what inputs are needed to drive it) and these process requirements may be described as *technical* in so far as the task of describing the process is bounded by rational measurable assumptions. However, when it comes to the output side (i.e. what reports the application should generate) then these decision support requirements may be described as *strategic* in so far as the task is not bounded by stable assumptions. For example, the user is being asked to make assumptions concerning individual roles, organisational policy, customer behaviour, market trends, and the identification of things and events outside of the scope of the defined process.

THE FAILURE OF ONLINE TRANSACTION PROCESSING (OLTP) TO PROVIDE A DECISION SUPPORT SYSTEM (DSS) CAPABILITY

The traditional conceptual components of an information system were inputs, processes and outputs. Because the focus of attention was on automating the process the concentration of effort was on the inputs which optimised the process. The outputs were a by-product of the exercise. This may be described as a 'functional orientation' which defines the function which is being automated and specifies what the system has to *do*. The real difficulty with this is that outputs cannot be bolted on to systems as they occur to users. It will normally be the case that key decisions on the design of the database will have made certain outputs difficult to combine and others almost impossible to provide without redesigning the database and/or the operational application.

In order to build as much flexibility into the application systems as was possible it became a standard practice in system development methodologies to separate the data from the process in the design of systems. A method is defined as an orderly or systematic procedure; a methodology is a set of methods and specific techniques, and the terms are frequently used interchangeably. This tendency was based on the premise that data remained very stable over time but that processes changed a great deal. This, of course, is substantially correct. For example, if you are a customer of a bank the data entities maintained on the computer system (e.g. customer, balance, account etc.) hardly change at all over long periods of time. The business process will change as changes are made to the way that the bank account operates (e.g. interest rates change, bank charges change, facilities on the account change etc). This view of the world was based on only two of the three components – input and process – the output component was not considered at all. However, it should be noted that a new approach to system design and programming – called the object oriented approach – is now emerging which reintegrates the data and the process when applications are being constructed and the data is, so to speak, 'wrapped around' the process.

Coupled with advances in user tools and graphical interfaces the object oriented systems will be far easier for users to access data. The fundamental flaws inherent in using transaction systems for decision support purposes – inappropriate data structures, data not integrated from different systems, coverage of data too short – will still obtain. But the problem of accessing standard control reports from functional systems will substantially diminish.

Of course, there has also been a traditional technology obstacle to providing an integrated view of data in an enterprise. This occurs because software engineers were trained and cultured at a time when machine resource (and peripheral equipment like disk packs) were expensive and the effort was directed at delivering an application which met the needs of the business process while minimising the technology costs. How this was done was for the software engineer to first establish what data was required to drive the process in the course of writing a functional specification for the system. Then the cheapest source for the data was identified, usually extracted from another system or a secondary source. Then the data was archived on to tapes as soon as the business process using the data had executed the tasks appropriate to the process. As applications expanded so too did the data problem. Soon the same data is resident in different systems, is inconsistent, has different attributes, belongs to different time bands, is unreconcilable or unavailable. This is the unavoidable legacy of a time when the focus of attention was in automating the business and reducing costs and where informating was a luxury that few organisations needed.

It should, of course, be conceded that the relative failure of corporate decision support systems cannot be attributed exclusively to the absence of an integrated store of corporate data. Failure can also be attributed to the development of inappropriate and inconsistent data models, parameters being based on incorrect assumptions, logical fallacies in the design of such systems and algorithmic differentials in the application program.

Observers of the information technology industry are fond of quoting the fact that the price performance of computer hardware has increased by sixteen orders of magnitude (10 000 000 000 000 000) while software development productivity has increased by only one order of magnitude in the same period. And most of that increase was achieved three decades ago when the first procedural programming languages replaced machine code. It is abundantly clear that something is dreadfully wrong and 'silver bullets' have been unveiled repeatedly to an increasingly cynical information systems community. This is all indicative of a science that is immature conceptually and which is evaluated continually from a technical perspective. The data warehouse will definitely not provide the conceptual elegance which the industry craves nor will it present orders of magnitude improvements in the productivity of software engineers. What it will achieve will be significant productivity gains among the ranks of knowledgeworkers whose productivity has held stubbornly static for the past two decades; but that achievement is no more than information systems have been doing for different categories of work since the first machine was deployed. If anything is significant about the data warehouse, over and above its place as part of the evolutionary continuum of information systems, it is that the data warehouse will transform not only the nature of work but the actual behaviour of markets.

A SHORT HISTORY OF THE DATABASE

In the beginning there was no concept of a 'database' or even of files. Where a computer program required data, it was embedded into the program. In order to cope with the larger volumes of data being encountered the concept of 'files' evolved. These were originally implemented on physical media such as punched paper tape or cards. In the 1970s magnetic tape became the standard medium for the storage of data. Later the magnetic disk pack made its entrance and the possibility of making large volumes of data available to the application programs allowed new kinds of application systems to be constructed. In these new applications, such as reservation systems, it was absolutely necessary to have up-to-date data available to the programs. File handling became refined over time as various techniques of indexation allowed files to be accessed at particular records rather than the entire file having to be read sequentially until the record was found. All the while, the physical file structures were tightly coupled to the application programs which read and updated the files. This led to two immediate problems. Firstly, each new use for existing data required a special new program to be written. Because it was an expensive and time-consuming event it effectively precluded the running of ad hoc queries. Secondly, in many cases the same data needed to be stored in more than one file, which in turn led to serious problems of synchronisation. So even if a special program was written for an ad hoc query, the result of the query might be wrong. This state of affairs was, needless to say, unsatisfactory.

The purpose of the database was to separate the application programs from the physical storage of the data. The database presents the application program with a logical view of the data. The database also handles many of the tiresome tasks associated with the physical storage of the data. By enabling different applications to store the same data, the schynronisation problems associated with the data were greatly reduced. In addition the database could be modified or extended without a great deal of modification to the application programs. Unhappily though, any significant changes to the application would result in mind-numbing modifications in the early database products.

The Hierarchical Database
The hierarchical model was the earliest type of database to be implemented and the most common hierarchical database product was IMS from IBM, which was introduced in 1968 and is still widely used for high-volume transaction processing applications to this day. One of the problems with the hierarchical database model is that the database has to be optimised for the application which uses the data. Therefore the problem of the data being held hostage by the application persisted, as did the need to write a complex computer program in order to satisfy the demand for an ad hoc query.

The Network Database
The network database model was a development of the hierarchical model and the most commonly implemented was the IDMS database from Cullinet. This model sought to alleviate the problem of multiple applications using the same data. This was achieved by using internal database pointers in order to connect two records where there was a logical relationship. At about this time (in the early 1970s) there was an attempt to introduce database standards through the work of the Conference on Data Systems Languages (Codasyl), the group which had successfully developed the Cobol computer programming language. However, this initiative languished and was overtaken by the more innovative relational model.

The Relational Database
The relational database model was successful because it took the separation of the data and the application one stage further. The relational database is, essentially, a series of two-dimensional tables comprising rows and columns. From the perspective of the business user this model makes the structure of the data considerably easier to understand. However, the big breakthrough for

decision support systems was that the relational database data manipulation language, SQL, quickly became an international standard. SQL (Structured Query Language) is a non-procedural language which cannot be used to write conventional programs but which is an extremely powerful tool when applied to the task of interrogating the database. While only a very few users will learn SQL, its benefit comes in terms of the productivity, consistency and transparency which it offers to the software engineers who are building the decision support system.

HARDWARE DEVELOPMENT

In the early 1950s it was estimated that 50 IBM Corporation model 704 mainframe computers would satisfy the computational requirements of the USA. Today, the processing capacity of a model 704 can be found on the desktop of a single knowledgeworker. The reason for the conservative (and wildly inaccurate) forecast was related to the enormously high cost of hardware in the 1950s.

However with the advent of solid state components such as transistors, and later of integrated circuits, the cost associated with building reliable computers tumbled. The introduction of 'virtual memory' made computers more efficient. The availability of disk storage devices made it possible for programs to accesss large volumes of data. And in the 1970s the microprocessor was born and with it all manner of computer processing became economically feasible.

Corporations may have sophisticated information systems at their disposal and yet experience severe information management problems. This can occur because different business units have, typically, built information systems without anticipating the need to integrate these systems with other corporate systems. Or it may have occurred because a corporation may have evolved through a series of takeovers and mergers and each original component had its own separate information systems. Or it may have occurred because a corporation may have lacked a comprehensive information systems architecture and so data definitions across different systems are incompatible. Or it may be that the competitive pressures on the business did not permit in-house information systems to be constructed and this factor forced business units to quickly adapt packaged solutions which will have led to an eclectic mix of systems and technologies. Or it may be that the corporation is utterly dependent on outdated legacy systems which have been amended to such an extent that the software is unstable and redesign is unthinkable.

Whatever the reason, most organisations have now arrived at this crisis. And unfortunately, most organisations have never needed data like they need it in today's turbulent markets.

THE FOUR FUNDAMENTAL OBSTACLES
IN THE CURRENT ENVIRONMENT

There were, however, four fundamental problems with building decision support systems which persisted in the world of information technology.

1. The Problem of Systems Integration

Firstly, there was occurring a 'disintegration' of enterprise information systems development where islands of automation sprung up in isolated and fragmented corporate initiatives. This happened for a number of reasons which fall in one of the following four categories.

(1) *Ownership* issues where functional sponsors of information systems were confined within organisational boundaries.

(2) *Planning* issues where it was decided to keep information systems design in manageable 'mindsized' chunks and where the design and development methodologies treated each system, (even similar systems like billing for different services), as separate independent projects.

(3) *Economic* issues where information systems were confined at an early stage to key activities, mainly financial, and then trickled out to other parts of the organisation as the cost of systems became affordable.

(4) *Organisational development* issues where enterprises evolved through a process of mergers and takeovers and where multiple information technology environments were combined.

2. The Problem of Hardware Architecture

The second problem had to do with the unchanged nature of the computer hardware architecture. Classical computer architecture was developed 40 years ago by John von Neumann at the Institute for Advanced Studies at Princeton, New Jersey. One of the central concepts of von Neumann's architecture was that control passes in a sequential fashion (unless explicitly modified) from one instruction to the next. What this implies is that routine transaction processing and complex queries cannot be run against the same image of the data without creating completely unpredictable and unacceptable variations in the performance of both activities. Even with the more recent advent of multiprocessor computers and parallel processor computers which depart significantly from the von Neumann principles the essential problem of partitioning these activities on a single machine remain, more or less, insoluble.

The individual performance patterns of the two environments are also completely different. In a transaction environment there are normally users who are updating information at terminals in a steady pattern of machine utilisation. Therefore the consumption of the computer resource may be said to be predictable. Where there are variations, for example when key punch operators go to lunch, the variation can be anticipated. On the other hand, the typical pattern of performance on a dedicated decision support system is completely unpredictable. A skilled user may execute a query which runs for a number of hours consuming all the available computer resource for that single user and the resource may remain idle for periods as no queries are run at all. This differential in utilisation patterns is identified in Figure 4.

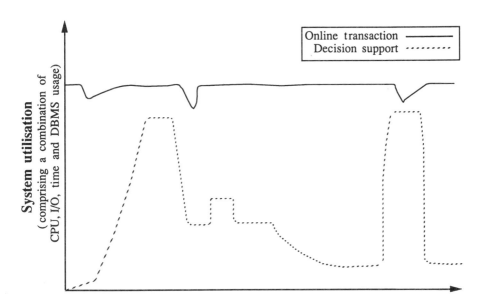

Figure 4 Different systems utilisation patterns for online transaction
systems and decision support systems

  The only possible means of combining both patterns of performance would be to schedule all queries to run overnight and dedicate the machine resource to the operational transaction users during normal working hours. This is not an ideal solution from a conceptual point of view since the characteristics of the data that a decision support user requires are radically different from the model used to support a transaction system. From a practical point of view this solution is generally not workable at all. In the case of billing systems, which tend to be the most in demand as a source of data for decision support systems, the machine resource is dedicated to transaction users punching up the data during the day and to batch processes which produce the bills overnight. The tendency in transaction systems has been for the window during which the machine is available for batch processing to shrink steadily from the point at which the system is introduced. This normally occurs because of routine batch processes such as backups, or because there may be specific batch processes built into the application (routines designed to update files), or because control reports have to be run overnight, or because the system may update another system. It is not uncommon for a user who has had a query program written to wait weeks for an opportunity for the program to be run, only to find on the appointed date that one of the scheduled batch programs has failed and has to be re-run. The query then goes back into the queue and the user waits all over again.

3. The Problem of Inconsistent Data

The third key problem relates to the difficulty in decoupling data from applications. In the traditional evolution of corporate information systems, data was modelled on the needs of individual departments in order to automate individual processes. Therefore, the data was inextricably bound up with the application and if the attributes of the data changed in any way, then the application programs would have to be amended. In addition, the data would not have had any real meaning outside of the requirements of the specific application.

In practice what this means is that similar data entities appear in multiple systems and there are multiple sources of record for these identical entities. In most instances none of the sources of record will describe the entity in precisely the same way, nor will the entities which have the same names mean the same thing. Therefore an entity called 'EMPLOYEE' may appear on a payroll system, a personnel system, a pensions system, a bonus scheme system, and an accounting system. A simple query such as 'How many people are working in a specific department?' is likely to elicit five different answers from the five systems. This is not because some systems are more accurate than others, nor because some systems have more competent administrators than others (although this is always a factor). In fact, each system will generate an answer to the query which is correct within the strict parameters of that system. For example, the payroll system may not include staff on secondments or sabbaticals; the pensions system may not include temporary or part time-staff who do not pay pension contributions; the bonus system may not include salaried staff not comprehended by the bonus scheme; the personnel system may not include contract or consultancy staff who are not employees of the enterprise. Therefore, the entity 'EMPLOYEE' has a different *semantic* meaning on each of the information systems. The question, How many people are working in the department? cannot be answered by any of the systems and the decision maker who posed the question will get back an answer from each of them which is precisely correct in the context of the individual systems. It will not, however, be precisely the answer to the question. This is extremely irritating. Some system administrators may berate the decision maker for being imprecise and for asking the wrong question! This is even more irritating.

In addition to the differences in the semantic meaning there will also be *syntactical* differences. These will occur because the data definitions on each of the systems are different. An attribute of EMPLOYEE called 'service' may mean the total years service in the company in the personnel system, and on the payroll system, and on the pensions system. But in each case the attribute is described differently. On one system it may be called 'service', but on another it may be called 'reckonable years' and on another it may be called 'total years'.

Add to these difficulties the fact that different systems archive data at different intervals, are resident on different technologies, and generate reports at week-end, at calendar month-end, at financial period-end etc. and some idea of the scale of the problem becomes evident. Therefore, when corporate decision makers dispute the accuracy of each other's data they are very often comparing apples with oranges. The result of all of this tight coupling of data with applications is the evolution of multiple, duplicate and redundant data stores which are difficult, costly and inefficient to maintain.

Add further to these difficulties the cultural problem that information systems personnel are generally unfamiliar with the business decisions which need support and the business users are generally unfamiliar with the structure and potential of the data to provide that support, and the broad canvas of the crisis becomes apparent.

4. The Problem of Data Pollution

One of the most frustrating problems which faces the designer of a decision support system and which will loom large in a data warehouse project relates to the quality of the data which resides on the operational systems. It is not that the data on the operational systems is invalid − the validity of the data has probably been checked by the system during the data entry stage. It is valid data, but it is valid junk data. Junk data tends to occur for one of three reasons.

Bad application design is one reason for the occurrence of junk data. Take, for example, the countless thousands of applications which offer the user a field with the option to enter 'male' or 'female' when the user does not wish to enter either of these options. How often is 'BUS' or 'business' or 'B' shoehorned into this field because there is nowhere else to record that this customer does not, in fact, have a gender but is a going commercial concern. Of course, when the original application was built there may only have been customers with genders and when the requirement arose later to provide for business customers it was not felt to be worth the effort to enhance the application. This author was amused to hear an insurance company executive relate the story of that company's claim processing system which regularly has inanimate objects such as 'lamp-post' or 'wall' entered as the third party in an accident. Here again the system designer may not have been entirely at fault since the insurance company may only have offered third party insurance when the system was designed and only decided later to offer comprehensive insurance. In yet another example, a hotel reservation system had a field reserved for car registration numbers which was also used to record passport numbers. Examples of data which has been corrupted and devalued by such practices are legion.

Ownership of application data is another reason why data becomes polluted and this occurs because data which is captured by an application in one area of the company is used by another area of the company and there is no compunction on the first area to quality assure the inputs for the end-user of the data. For example, it is common in information systems for order processing applications (which reside in the sales department) to be used as the vehicle to capture marketing data. Therefore the order processing clerk gets an order and keys it in at the counter for a customer. The customer is (naturally) in a hurry and the clerk may also be under some pressure. When the screen that seeks data inputs on subjects such as 'industry category' or 'size of enterprise' or 'how did you find out about our product?' the sales clerk may enter any convenient code that enters his or her head. After all it doesn't matter to the sales transaction; it is only used by some anonymous department in head office. And it may not be the fault of the sales clerk because the person placing the order may be an intermediary or a courier who would not have the information. In any event there is no compelling reason why the sales clerk should go to any trouble to assure the accuracy of the data or to seek to alter the procedure for gathering this data. Back in head office the marketing gurus are spending a small fortune on an exciting new target marketing and discounting promotion to an industry sector which has never used the services of the company.

The *absence of standard data entry naming conventions* is not so much a problem of polluted data as data which has been inconsistently entered. The most common example of this category may be found in the simple matter of the name of a customer. Let us say, for example, that the customer is a nationwide retail company called 'Nationwide Sales Corporation Limited' trading as 'The Shopping Emporium'. Straightaway the customer will appear as 'Nationwide Sales Corporation Limited' and as 'The Shopping Emporium'. But the chances are that it will also appear as 'NSC Limited', 'NSC', 'NSC Ltd.', 'Nationwide Sales Corp.', 'TSM', 'THE SHOPPING EMPOR.', and any other combination of upper and lower case abbreviations which can possibly be entered on the available fields. This problem becomes more acute when subsidiaries of companies are involved and it is increasingly important to see the customer as a single entity comprising the full range of services being consumed by all of the related companies. What this requires at a system level is the ability to have a super-type 'Customer' with multiple sub-types and to specify and enforce a standard naming convention for customers who have multiple accounts at multiple locations.

Cleaning up polluted data may prove easy or difficult depending on the scale and nature of the contamination. In a mild case of data pollution it is usually possible when mapping the data from source to target environments to make the necessary adjustments to ensure that the semantic meaning of the data is coherent and consistent. Often it is simply a matter of running a 'find and replace' program against the data in the operational system in order to apply a standard naming convention to a customer or an event. However, in more severe cases the level of contamination may be such that there is no point in proceeding with a data warehouse until such time as the issue of data quality can be addressed. When considering the issues associated with this topic it is essential, even axiomatic, to resolve at the outset to tackle the process which has given rise to the junk data rather than being tempted into a once-off clean-up of the available data. Always remember that the operational systems are the systems of record in the enterprise and the data warehouse should not be used as a means of hiding or correcting deficiencies in the operational systems.

RESPONSES TO THE CRISIS

The information technology industry has responded to the crisis with many point solutions, none of which responds in a fundamental sense to the demands of the business. However, all of the point solutions comprise some part of the overall solution and there will be a high degree of convergence of many of the principles of these solutions in the application of the data warehouse computing environment.

Decentralised Processing
Some organisations have decentralised the data processing activity so that the data is nearer to the end-users and that the organisation can exploit the more recent price/performance benefits of smaller computers and in the earnest hope that distributed database technology matures quickly. This is essentially a variation on 'explaining the problem to the client' – it is 'handing the problem to the client'. The fact that the business user now owns the problem does mean that they will stop complaining about it in the short term, but the problem will be revisited upon the enterprise in a more virulent form. In organisations which have adopted this model the integration of corporate data has, more than likely, been pushed further into the future. It should be noted that there is a key difference here between decentralising the applications (which is feasible and increasingly desirable) and fragmenting the data.

Extract Processing
Extract processing is a phenomenon which has mushroomed with the growth of departmental computers and more recently with personal computers. Now everyone who possesses a PC wants to have their own personal database or spreadsheet populated by data from some corporate system. And so there

proliferate thousands of corporate databases based on thousands of different specifications, all sharing and exchanging data as extracts of extracts are merged with other extracts to generate ever more pure degrees of corporate nonsense.

Executive Information Systems (EIS)

Executive information systems is a response to the needs of senior managers to have some kind of access to integrated data at a high level of aggregation. Most EIS systems contain a relatively small database and easy-to-use access is provided for the senior executive to the graphical depiction of the information through the use of point and click techniques or touch-sensitive screens. EIS systems provide a benefit to the business in terms of focusing on key indices of performance and are, in essence, executive control tools. Because there is nothing substantial behind the EIS system there cannot be any real facility to 'drill down' into the information since the prepackaged information is normally cobbled together by software conjurers who combine the data from file transfers, printouts, tapes and diskettes. It is the illusion of integration painstakingly pieced together – the triumph of style over substance.

Corporate Planning Models

Many useful models have been developed for corporate planning and most of these models require to be populated with data from the operational systems. These models are then analysed iteratively over a multi-year planning horizon. Because of the volumes of data which are processed by large corporations it is necessary to automate some elements of this analysis activity. One of the difficulties with such models is that all of the planning activities in the enterprise (corporate planning, functional planning, regional planning product planning, information technology planning etc.) should be using the same source data, and this is not always the case unless the lower-order models are subsets of the higher-order model.

Expert Systems

Expert Systems (also known as knowledge based systems, an offshoot of artificial intelligence) enjoyed a brief vogue at the end of the 1980s but has proved to be premature for commercial applications. Expert systems are constructed using specialised application languages and the application is driven by 'rules'. The rules are normally derived from a human expert and these may include uncertainties which are normally expressed as percentages. The user of an expert system answers questions that the system poses and by accumulating information from the user the system will guide him or her to an appropriate decision. Because of the interrogatory nature of the interaction of such systems it is primarily in the realm of professional diagnosis (technical, medical, legal, financial) that expert systems have enjoyed success.

In the long run the introduction of artificial intelligence will make information systems more *cybernetic* in so far as the systems will be able to reason, learn and make judgements. But this intelligence in expert systems exists only at a most rudimentary level. When the expert system encounters data, the system cannot perceive any pattern in the data unless it has been provided with rules to apply to the data. And these rules have to be supplied by a human expert. Because most expert systems are designed to be *decision making* (and therefore designed to replace the human expert in some mechanistic field of endeavour) rather than *decision aiding* (designed to enhance the natural ability of the decision maker in a creative field of endeavour) the expert system is an information technology solution to a structured problem which can be easily specified rather than to unstructured or ad hoc conditions.

Query Tools

User query tools have been developed by a number of suppliers and are used by business users as tools to access data locked up in corporate databases. Some of these tools are quite sophisticated and can be used to access data in many different computer environments and are often capable of presenting many different data formats in relational views *(transparency software)* but ultimately this approach suffers from the deficiencies evident in the fundamental problems discussed earlier. The query tools require considerable training, the user will be unfamiliar with the structure of the data in the target environment, the query tools are notoriously processor intensive and the users will impact dramatically on the online response times. In addition much of the data the user requires may be archived and not available on the system.

Relational Databases/SQL

The relational database was to have been something of a panacea for decision makers who required easy access to data. Relational databases are different from previously database structures because the logical structure of the data is in simple two-dimensional tables.. This structure is easier to comprehend and this combined with the availability of the powerful non-procedural Structured Query Language (SQL) held out the promise that data was at last going to be accessible. It should be noted that SQL is not a computer language in the conventional sense, because it cannot be used to develop application programmes. SQL is an extremely flexible relational database manipulation language. The advent of relational databases and SQL were extremely good news for application developers but for users it was a tantilising disappointment. No database administrator was going to let SQL into the hands of users because all of the fundamental problems still existed. The online response time performance of the production system could be threatened by users running ad hoc queries; users would still not understand the semantic and syntactical meaning of the data and SQL, while not a very complex tool, is still a software tool for computer professionals. The relational database was to be the gateway to data and SQL was to be the means of access. The former couldn't; the latter wasn't.

Conclusion

Different systems which reside in the world of decision support have different characteristics and have a different purpose. Most decision support software systems for problem solving are defined in terms of the *system objectives* and orientation. Executive information systems are normally defined in terms of the *interface characteristics* of the system. Management information systems which provide a reporting facility (typically a transaction system with relational database facilities) are normally defined in terms of the *system capabilities and utilities.* Report processing software tools are normally defined in terms of the *functional richness* of the reporting tools. Artificial intelligence applications are normally defined in terms of the *expert knowledge* of the system. The   corporate data warehouse is different since it is properly defined in the context of an information technology *architecture* rather than an application.

A HISTORY OF DECISION SUPPORT SYSTEMS FRAMEWORKS

A good deal of confusion has traditionally obtained about the definitions of MIS and DSS and the currency of *information* has been devalued considerably by an industry which has proclaimed the 'Age of Information' at the launch of every hardware and software innovation in the last thirty years.

The appropriate characteristics of a DSS have been explained extensively by academic commentators and these debates have centred on whether the system supports models or simply displays data; or whether the system supports only repetitive 'canned' queries or supports ad hoc queries; or whether the nature of the decision making being supported is 'operational' or 'strategic'. What these debates were actually concerned with was weighing the relative importance of the different constraints which applied to existing DSS. Mark S. Silver provides a good summary of this debate and opts sensibly for the following broad-based definition: 'A Decision Support System is a computer based information system that affects or is intended to affect how people make decisions'. [10]

So, is the data warehouse the latest and most exciting manifestation of decision support systems ? Well, in the opinion of this author, it is not a decision support system at all. It is something altogether more fundamental. It is the means – the base infrastructure – by which decision support systems can be built. In this new architecture the data warehouse is simply a pool of integrated and enriched corporate data which can be used as a database server to multiple clients, and the actual decision support systems will be resident on these clients. Of course, in the absence of any decision support applications a user may execute a query on the data warehouse and the result of the query will undoubtedly enhance decision making. But this is to miss the point. In this example the query becomes a single executable (and disposable) decision support application. *It is the query that supports decision making, not the data warehouse.* A more sophisticated application than the once-off query might be a sophisticated simulation model for 'What If' analysis. This application might fire off multiple requests for data to the data warehouse and execute complex computational algorithms. The point of the data warehouse is to enable such applications. In the same way that online transaction applications could not be constructed without the existence of a data communications infrastructure, the deployment of decision support systems will fail to achieve their potential (or will simply not be possible to conceive) in the absence of a corporate data warehouse.

> Therefore, the definition of the data warehouse which is proposed is: *A corporate data warehouse is a single integrated store of data which provides the infrastructural basis for informational software applications in the enterprise.*

The data warehouse is the gateway which separates the world of operational processing from the world of decision support applications. The operational world will comprise a legacy of many information systems which were introduced with a focus on making the enterprise more efficient and cost-effective. These systems will have large numbers of users sitting at visual display units inputting data and these systems will reside in particular functions of the enterprise. It is the data from these systems which will be used to build a new generation of systems where the focus will be on managing a more effective enterprise. This is illustrated in Figure 5.

One distinguishing feature of data pattern analysis on a data warehouse from previous DSS applications is that traditional DSS *enhanced* the knowledge of the decision maker while the data warehouse *supplements* the knowledge of the decision maker.

Herbert Simon first identified the distinction between 'programmed' and 'non-programmed' decisions. 'Decisions', according to Simon, 'are non-programmed to the extent that they are novel, unstructured and consequential'. [11]

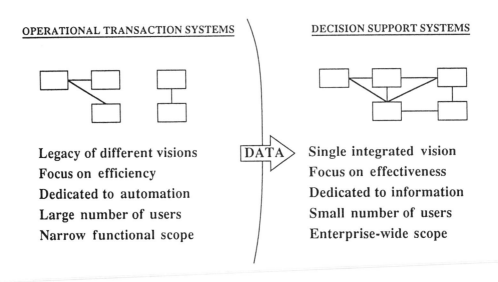

OPERATIONAL TRANSACTION SYSTEMS   DECISION SUPPORT SYSTEMS

Legacy of different visions   DATA   Single integrated vision
Focus on efficiency   Focus on effectiveness
Dedicated to automation   Dedicated to information
Large number of users   Small number of users
Narrow functional scope   Enterprise-wide scope

Figure 5 - The evolving IT architecture of separate application domains

After Simon had published his definition a widely accepted taxonomy was developed by Robert Anthony [12] who described three categories of managerial activity. These were *operational control* (which is concerned with the execution of tasks and is highly structured), *management control* (which is concerned with the supervision of those engaged in carrying out the tasks) and *strategic planning* (which is concerned with deciding on the objectives of the organisation and deploying resources in pursuit of those objectives).

Gorry and Scott-Morton [13] in their seminal paper on information systems defined further the difference between structured and unstructured decision making. Gorry and Scott-Morton observed that Anthony's three levels of managerial activity equated to structured (operational control), semi-structured (management control) and unstructured (strategic planning) activities and rejected the idea, common in the 1960s, of a 'total systems approach' to meeting the needs of all of these activities. Structured decision making was consigned by Gorry and Scott-Morton to the world of Management Information Systems (MIS) which produced pre-defined reports at pre-defined intervals. Unstructured decisions were located within the Gorry and Scott-Morton framework in a new information systems environment which they called Decision Support System (DSS). They also noted that the skills required in this new environment would be distinctly different from those required in the MIS world.

In a retrospective commentary on their original treatise [14] both authors reiterated their conviction that a decision centred view of an organisation remains a valid means for providing the basis for information technology development. But, significantly, they expressed the wish to substitute the term 'tactical planning' for 'management control'. This is significant in so far as it had become more clear in the 1980s that the pace of change in industry, the turbulence of international markets and the intensity of competition was blurring the distinction between routine middle management control (reactive) and planning (proactive) activities. The idea that all planning activities were long-term or the sole responsibility of senior executives has, in the meantime, come and gone.

With regard to the dichotomy between routine and ad hoc queries, it should be stated that it will be the goal of most corporations to capture creative and valuable ad hoc queries and convert them into re-usable applications. This process of routinising decision support and embedding it at lower levels in the organisation will occur over time. Therefore, what is likely to occur is that in the beginning there will be ad hoc applications generated by the few, which over time, will become decision support applications utilised by the many. To use a mining analogy, ad hoc queries can be compared to prospecting for ore, while structured applications can be compared to full-scale production. The one must precede the other.

The Gorry and Scott-Morton framework has remained dominant in the field of decision support systems and has many improvers, most of whom accept the distinction between operational decision support with its routine and specific requirements, and strategic decision support with its unique and ad hoc requirements. There is also general agreement on the need to construct DSS applications in iterative cycles. And finally, there is general agreement that there is an absolute need to populate DSS applications with corporate data, with various disagreements on the level of granularity required for such systems.

Silver identifies two key characteristics which should be carefully considered before embarking on the design of a decision support system. The first characteristic is that the decision making activity does not occur at the moment of choice and that it is, in fact, 'a complex sequence of differentiated activities occurring over time'. [15] The second characteristic is that numerous distinct paths may be followed in order to arrive at a decision and that 'choosing the path (determining the structure of the process) is more important and more difficult than traversing it (executing the process)'. [16] Therefore it can be asserted that the pursuit of a decision is neither intuitive nor automatic nor instant and is essentially an exploratory and iterative process impacted by a high degree of prejudice and accident. This gives the lie to assertions that rigorous specifications for decision support systems can be produced in advance of the design. Users need to discover their requirements by interacting with the data. Where specifications are produced the applications will be arid and artificial. Silver's second characteristic – that the structure of the process is more important than executing the process – gives the lie to the assertion that all that the user requires is access to the data. Unrestricted access without the assistance of some structured applications will only result in the user drowning in the sea of data.

One of the key features of most DSS applications which have been deployed is the heuristic character of the human-software interface. Heuristic is a word which has its origins in a Greek word meaning 'to invent' and 'to discover'. Heuristics can be a particularly valuable means of exploring data in a poorly defined and unstructured environment or in the absence of a specific, defined problem.

Much of the commentary on the nature, impact and value of DSS applications has focused, in the past, on software systems designed to support the decision maker. This, of course, is only natural. However, DSS software is of no benefit to a decision maker if it requires inputs that the decision maker does not have. Benefit only accrues to the decision maker when he or she can utilise the decision support software to process relevant data to produce information. In the absence of comprehensive and accurate data, a decision support system is just an empty shell. And, in the absence of appropriate decision support applications, the data warehouse is a monolithic and inert pool of data. Individual operational DSS applications can be populated by small-scale extract processing, but genuinely strategic decision support will require a fully functioning data warehouse. It will be most valued by corporations most in need of real-time strategy – those enterprises which are operating in an environment of constant flux. And, among this growing constituency of enterprises, strategic error is invariably fatal.

It is important to emphasise that the data warehouse is a technological solution to a business problem. The centralisation of data and the physical and logical segregation of operational and informational data is driven, not by any elegant theoretical reason, but by the constraints of the existing technology. The realm of information technology has proved a treacherous territory for researchers and scholars who have searched for unifying theoretical frameworks to explain or influence the software development environment. Very often the software engineers under scholarly scrutiny were not acting in the manner observed because of any rational instinct but because of the constraints of the technology. Therefore, as the technology continues to evolve on a number of separate planes there is a high degree of unpredictable change occurring in separate domains. Within this evolving state the potential of the data warehouse to be used to launch other informational applications will not be lost on astute software engineers but can only be realised where the first application is based on a robust enterprise-wide data model.

In general terms there are, at present, two key assumptions associated with our understanding of decision support systems which require to be probed more vigorously. They are :

(1)   The symmetric (and synthetic) assumption that operational data used to support operational decisions is resident on operational transaction systems and that strategic data (normally aggregate data) is used to supportstrategic decision making. This may be flawed by the blurred line dividing these domains and the need to navigate from general (summary) to particular (detailed) data on a   single integrated database.

(2)   The assumption that decision support systems are primarily directed at 'problem solving'. In this scheme of things there must first be a visible and defined 'problem'. After a decision support system has been brought to bear on this problem, there will hopefully be a 'solution'. This is a neat, but synthetic, view of corporate decision making. The actual conditions which obtain in most enterprises are different. It is likely that there is no visible overt 'problem', and that instead that there are invisible threats and opportunities which the decision maker is unaware of. Making the decision maker aware of these conditions will enable him or her to adapt the posture of the enterprise in a manner which enables the enterprise to evade the threat and seize the opportunity.

CONCLUSION

Any architecture which allocates those systems concerned with processes into one domain and those concerned with decisions into another has formed the basis for constructing the new informating applications, but also runs the risk of building artificial barriers between the two environments. Therefore, it is necessary to state that, in the context of the data warehouse, these two domains belong to a single holistic architecture. Each may have its own distinct characteristics and goals. But it is a bipolar architecture with data as the unifying dynamic. As a consequence, it is true to observe that, when one pole is subjected to change, the other, by definition, does not escape the consequences of that change. For example, changes in the transaction systems in the operational domain will impact on the data migration software that bridges the two computing environments. Likewise, insights gained by the data warehouse applications will precipitate changes in the business which will require alterations to the operational transaction systems.

Chapter 5
Defining the Business Requirements: Building an Enterprise Model

Before embarking on a project to design and build a corporate decision support system it will first be necessary to define the information requirements of the enterprise *as a whole*. This can be done by attempting to describe the business at an enterprise level in terms of its information characteristics. This description of the enterprise needs to be framed in a manner that can be easily understood and updated and this is what the 'enterprise model' seeks to do.

THE ENTERPRISE MODEL: A DESCRIPTION

An enterprise model will comprise a number of separate models which, combined together, provide an integrated picture of the enterprise. There may be many of these separate models which describe the enterprise in terms of enterprise strategy, enterprise organisation, enterprise data, enterprise processes, or enterprise culture. It is essential that the enterprise model captures a holistic view of the enterprise and is not confined only to systems since the appropriate alignment between the business *and* the systems is one of the key goals of the endeavour. The enterprise model itself may be divided into sub-models which describe different functions in a corporation and are sometimes referred to as 'subject area' models. These subject area models represent a more detailed description of the enterprise at departmental level. The subject areas are set out diagrammatically in Figure 6.

For the software engineer all of the components of the enterprise model will be important but the two outputs that will be input directly into an information systems development project are (a) a *corporate process model* and (b) a

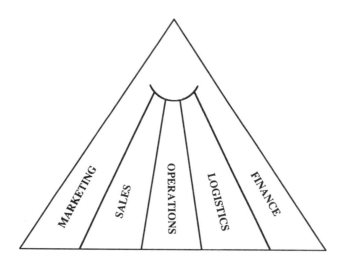

Figure 6 - Functionally segmented enterprise subject-areas

corporate data model. A corporate process model is a structured description of the elementary processes in the enterprise which identifies the inter-relationships between the different processes. A typical process in a commercial enterprise would be the process of billing customers for goods or services. A corporate data model is a description of the data 'entities' which are generated by (or required by) the elementary processes that are carried out by the enterprise. In an elementary process, like billing, the process requires that data about certain entities exist such as 'customer', 'order', 'product' etc. and the process will generate data such as invoice', 'payment record', 'credit terms' etc. From the specific perspective of designing a data warehouse, it is the corporate data model which will be of critical importance; but the data model will only be truly useful and 'futureproof' if it is validated by the other models, especially by the process model and the strategy model.

THE ORIGIN OF ENTERPRISE MODELLING

The origin of most of the enterprise analysis methodologies available today have their roots either in Information Engineering (IE) which was developed by James Martin or in the Business System Planning (BSP) methodology developed by IBM. Both IE and BSP emerged in the 1970s as a means of providing a rigorous framework for what was, and is, a daunting task. Today both IE and BSP have been updated and re-packaged by their originators, and many improvers and imitators have developed products which have different strengths and weaknesses in different circumstances. But all methods have in common the goal of capturing the relationships between the processes in a business and the data required by or generated by these processes.

However, it is crucially important when discussing information engineering in the context of the data warehouse to distinguish between the long term business goal of information engineering, which is to *integrate all of the operational systems* in the enterprise, and the short-term business goal of the data warehouse, which is to *integrate the enterprise data* required to support decision making in the enterprise.

Information engineering was described by James Martin as, an interlocking set of formal techniques in which enterprise models, process models and data models are used to create and maintain data processing systems.

It is instructive, and not a little unsettling, to observe a passage from an article by Dr William Zani in a 1970 issue of the Harvard Business Review which was quoted in the introduction to the original BSP manual and which is reproduced here :

' Traditionally, management information systems have not really been designed at all. They have been spun off as by-products while improving existing systems within a company. No tool has proved so disappointing in use. I trace this disappointment to the fact that most management information systems have been developed in the bottom-up fashion – an effective system, under normal conditions, can only be born of a carefully planned , rational design that looks down from the top, the natural vantage point of the managers who will use it. [17]

BSP set out to reverse the 'bottom-up' tendency in information systems design and the advent of methodologies advocating the 'top-down' approach have been experiencing considerable, but by no means extensive, success. The problem with the 'bottom-up' approach, when it comes to defining the requirements of decision makers, is that the data which would seem to the 'top-down' manager to be an obvious component of the system may simply not be there at all. This occurs because no account was taken when the system was built of the needs of decision makers and the system is devoted only to the automation of an isolated process. Although it is dedicated to the transformation of a complex and diverse data maze into a coherent information grid and can even, in some circumstances, derive new items of data by combining and manipulating existing data, the data warehouse cannot generate what does not exist and what cannot be derived, replicated, or extrapolated from an existing data source. The vision of BSP as expressed by IBM was to enable businesses to 'consolidate the key data files and make information available not just to individual functions or departments but throughout the business, in order for management to gain an overall view of the business and be able to take multi-functional decisions'. This remains the goal of most enterprise analysis methodologies and is a key objective of most corporate information systems plans. So, most businesses (especially the large corporations) have seen the light and maintain comprehensive enterprise models? Well no, this does nor appear to be the case. Most studies of the state of software development indicate that a majority are still at a very early stage in the application of structured techniques at the level of the enterprise.

What most organisations have done in the past is to analyse business processes with a view to automating them and the sum total of these processes represents the actual enterprise model of the organisation. Until quite recently, most of the methodologies employed by software engineers commenced at a stage called *analysis*, proceeded to a stage called *design* and then concluded with a stage called *construction*. Most of the inputs and outputs in the methodological process assumed either that the business process being computerised was independent of everything else in the world (which was dishonest) or glibly assumed that a valid high-level enterprise model existed in the organisation which provided some inputs to the analysis stage (which was naive).

In most organisations it is unlikely that any coherent corporate data model exists at all since data is simply a by-product of the 'disintegrated' business processes. This actual model of corporate information systems architecture is normally a chaotic agglomeration of different systems with gaps, duplication, overlaps, and redundancy evident from every perspective. For example, many corporations have separate personnel systems, payroll systems and pensions systems which have been developed on entirely different principles to support separate business processes which are not organically linked. Most organisations have a multitude of different billing systems for the different services which they offer but are incapable of linking these systems together to provide a common view of a customer who uses the different services.

This phenomenon has *two* separate negative impacts on the enterprise. Firstly, the business processes which should be linked are not, and this leads in many instances to chronic dysfunction embedded in these processes. Secondly, this traditional evolution of corporate information systems has occurred in a fashion which has optimised the impact of technology on individual business processes at the expense of managing the entire body of corporate data in a coherent manner. Both of these negative impacts can be addressed by constructing an enterprise model and migrating the existing *actual model* progressively towards the *ideal model* which will itself be a moving target.

THE ENTERPRISE MODEL AND BUSINESS PROCESS RE-ENGINEERING

Many readers will be familiar with the anecdote of the railway company which extolled the mission to be 'the best long-distance railway company in the world'. Because they remained faithful to this mission they succeeded in achieving it, but it was cold comfort for them when they slipped into commercial oblivion and realised that they had never been in the railway business. They had, of course, been in the transportation business.

Because of the potential for confusion about the mission and goals of an enterprise it is essential that the objects of the strategy model element of the enterprise model are clearly associated with the data and process models. For example, it is important to know what the key information needs of particular corporate goals are because these goals may change or be superseded by new goals. The applications that access the data in the data warehouse must be constructed on the basis that they are, to some extent, 'futureproofed'.

The pursuit of the radical transformation of business processes has become the dominant theme of management endeavour in the nineties. One of the reasons for the popularity of business process re-engineering (BPR) is related to the same phenomenon which is encountered in the data warehouse project, namely the need to re-integrate the business. The end-result of many (if not all) BPR exercises is to simplify the business process. BPR is a recognition that a huge level of wasteful activity occurs in the enterprise because of the disaggregated nature of elementary business processes. It is an interesting subject of debate whether elementary business processes became disaggregated in the first instance because of the limitations of information systems in comprehending the full complexity of the entire process or whether information systems simply mirrored disjointed organisational structures which had already divided processes into synthetic units of production. Whichever is the case, it is clear that common ground will be traversed by BPR and data warehouse analysts. Both endeavours are directed at perceiving a holistic and integrated whole from the sum of the disjointed parts which comprise the typical modern enterprise. Both are concerned with the identification and simplification of core processes. In the BPR project these processes will invariably be in the operational domain of the enterprise and will be production or service delivery oriented, i.e. transaction-based processes. In the data warehouse projects the same core business processes will also be under scrutiny but attention will be focused on the strategy formulation domain of the enterprise, i.e. decision making processes. In this sense BPR and the data warehouse are quite separate initiatives and one is in no way a substitute for the other. The common denominator in both cases is likely to be the 'customer' and 'product' entities. The data warehouse will be directed at optimising strategy and BPR will be directed at optimising the operational process required to implement that strategy.

Because so many of the analysis tools and techniques as well as the end products of the analysis have a good deal in common it would be prudent, where both initiatives are ongoing in the enterprise, to carefully co-ordinate both projects. At a practical level it will be extremely irritating for key executives and knowledgeworkers to be visited by two sets of analysts pursuing an apparently similar agenda. At a more serious level it would be disastrous if two separate and competing enterprise models were to emerge within the enterprise.

There are two stages during the data warehouse project which present opportunity checkpoints to directly input to the BPR project. These occur at the pre-deployment stage when requirements are being specified and at the post-deployment stage when decision support applications are being utilised by the business.

In the pre-deployment (analysis) stage of the data warehouse project, opportunities will be presented for the redesign of the business processes under consideration. This will, in most cases, be identified in the strategy sub-model of the enterprise model and will come to light because of dysfunctional links in the association matrices. For example, if key decision making processes require data which does not exist in the enterprise, or if there is no clear linkage between the corporate mission and goals of individual functions, or where there is fundamental disagreement among decision makers on the decision support needs of the enterprise business process, then it is clear that there is a need for a more radical level of analysis. This activity belongs more properly to the BPR project. Of course, where no specific BPR project exists then the data warehouse team and project sponsor will have to grapple with the issues presented and attempt to resolve the contradictions within the scope of the data warehouse project.

In the post-deployment stage of the data warehouse project it is almost inevitable that the decision support applications will quickly identify potential new strategies for the enterprise. These strategies may be presented as threats or opportunities and will immediately bring pressure to bear on the operational business processes (and the operational information systems which support these processes) to implement the new strategies. For example, it will be quite common for the data warehouse to be utilised by the marketing function in order to identify nested layers of customer segments. It will be equally common for the marketing function to the use the data warehouse to construct a pricing model which can then be applied to these segments. The end-result might be a complex discounting package tailored to individual customer segments. Then it becomes clear that the operational business processes, especially the customer billing process, would be incapable of supporting this new package. In this example the data warehouse is becoming a key driver of process redesign in the business, and this is likely to be a common feature of data warehouse implementations.

THE DATA WAREHOUSE AND THE ENTERPRISE MODEL

The long-term positive impact that the enterprise model will have on the enterprise is the integration of the business processes, and this will occur through the redesign of the processes themselves and of the information systems which support those processes. However, most organisations cannot wait until the business processes are fully integrated and want an integrated view of the data available *now*. The enterprise model can deliver a short-term positive impact on the enterprise by *integrating the data*. This presents an opportunity to the enterprise to offload data from the 'disintegrated' current model on to a data warehouse type platform which can integrate the data according to the corporate data model contained in the enterprise model. Now the enterprise has achieved the benefits of the integrated data model before the longer-term (and more expensive) goal of integrating the process model.

This is simply a recognition that the means to *plan* must exist before the means of *delivery* is made available.

Whether an organisation builds an enterprise model before proceeding to construct a data warehouse essentially depends on whether the data architecture in the warehouse is going to be constructed on the basis of a top-down approach (based on the enterprise model) or whether it is based on the bottom-up approach (based on whatever is available and accessible in the operational systems). This marks an essential decision which will impact on the nature and functionality of the delivered data warehouse. A top-down approach implies a strategic, as opposed to an operational, perspective of the data and this may fundamentally impact on the ability of the applications to deliver value in either a strategic or operational domain. This will be important to bear in mind when considering the issue of organisational alignment which is examined later in the book. Of course this is a slightly exaggerated view of the alternatives. In practice, even with the benefit of an enterprise model, there will be substantial gaps between what is ideal, what is feasible and what is implemented. While there should be a boundary around the enterprise architecture beyond which the system designer should not stray, the enterprise model should not be represented as a panacea or as a rigid target for the development of informating applications. Because, in the real world, there will be resource constraints, technology constraints, design constraints and the usual unreasonable demands of the business, choices will have to be made between effective short-term solutions and optimum long-term solutions. The real immediate benefit of the enterprise model is to offer a consistent frame of reference within which to make decisions on the trade-offs between various design options.

A different, and altogether more strategic, benefit in using the enterprise model in building the corporate data warehouse is to use the relational schema of the data in the warehouse environment as a basis for redesigning the operational systems and thereby use the data warehouse as a means of accelerating the introduction of the integrated *business process* model.

As with the data warehouse the construction of an enterprise model is a pan-corporate project. Like the data warehouse the enterprise model is attempting to take a holistic view of the corporation. Like the data warehouse the enterprise model is a strategic investment and both projects will seem to promise intangible rather than tangible benefits. Like the data warehouse the enterprise model is likely to have a severe impact on organisational processes and structures.

However, an organisation can build a data warehouse without having an enterprise model. In this regard, two particular assertions must be considered carefully. Firstly, the construction of an enterprise model, however rigourous and comprehensive the model, will not solve the problem of integrating the data on operational systems. This is an important point to note since some observers see the enterprise model as an alternative to building a data warehouse. Secondly, it is not necessary to construct an enterprise model before proceeding to build a data warehouse and many developers have arrived at 80:20 data warehouse solutions without the more elegant design framework of an enterprise model. The synergies which might accrue from combining both initiatives under the supervision of the same corporate sponsor should be seriously considered. Many organisations baulk at the task of constructing an enterprise model and this reluctance is explained by three separate reasons.

(1) Organisations plead that there is too much change generated by organisational, economic and competitive uncertainty, and that there would be no single point in time when the model would be accurate.
(2) Some senior executives are wary of constructing an enterprise model because it is likely to identify all kinds of deficiencies in the enterprise which would be potentially damaging to individuals or groups and because there is a tendency to precipitate the redesign of business processes which often has the effect of disrupting existing power structures.
(3) Information systems personnel, under increasing pressure to deliver systems, do not feel that the resources can be diverted to an activity that does not actually ship software.

Building the enterprise model is typically a case of having the courage to put the important before the urgent. It is precisely because there is change and turbulence in the business and poor productivity in the information technology function that the enterprise model should be built. The primary cause of systems failing to meet the expectations of users during the 1980s had to do with information systems not being properly aligned with the business that they were supporting. In many ways the enterprise model is an agreed charter which is arrived at jointly by the business users of information systems and by the designers of the information systems and which navigates a course for the future.

INTEGRATING THE ENTERPRISE

The key concept which motivates an organisation to construct an enterprise model and to devise corporate software standards is the concept of integration. Integration needs to occur on three separate axes.

Firstly, there is *horizontal integration* which is the integration of all of the components of an individual application. This is the most basic form of integration since it seeks only to ensure that the application that is being constructed is fully integrated within its own boundaries and that there are no inconsistencies in the final software product. This level of integration may be achieved without reference to an enterprise model and serves only to build quality into isolated applications.

Secondly, there is *vertical integration* which is found less frequently in enterprises and is the means whereby the application designer ensures that the application is congruent with the business requirement. In order to ensure that the software application is correctly aligned with the business it is necessary to have the high-level model of the enterprise (especially the strategy component of the enterprise model) tightly coupled with the individual applications. In this way the software that is constructed to automate a particular business process is validated against the mission, goals, objectives and critical success factors of the enterprise. Vertical integration of an application requires some level of enterprise analysis to have occurred but it will be necessary to ensure the vertical integration of an application for the enterprise modelling to have been confined to a subject-area.

Finally, there is *enterprise integration* which seeks to provide consistent definitions of data and processes across the enterprise. To arrive at a comprehensive enterprise model the enterprise will need to engage in a purification of all of the naming conventions used to describe objects in the enterprise as well as a clarification of the definitions of these objects. Therefore the data and activities which occur in an enterprise and the interactions between them throughout the enterprise can be standardised. This can only be achieved by constructing a comprehensive enterprise model (a) which has been validated by the business users of the information systems in the enterprise and (b) where strict compliance with the model is observed by all software engineers working in (or for) the enterprise.

THE ENTERPRISE MODEL AND OPERATIONAL INFORMATION SYSTEMS

Most methodologies which are used to construct an enterprise model address the later stages in the lifecycle of engineering a software application. These subsequent stages in the lifecycle which are supported by the methodology and which are normally included are the analysis, design and construction stages. Some methodologies will also address the testing and maintenance stages but these are less common at present. Each of these stages will normally be supported by a software tool which is used to store the information gathered at each stage and which may be used to retrieve information, to cross-reference information, to generate diagrams or to provide automated support for the different analysis techniques which are embodied in the methodology. This automation of the methodology is commonly referred to as CASE (Computer-Aided Software Engineering) and it will be possible quite soon through the use of CASE tools to automate the entire process of writing computer programs. The benefits of a CASE environment will be experienced largely in the area of higher quality and productivity and integration in the development of operational process-oriented applications. However, the central store of information about the data in the enterprise (called 'metadata') will be stored in CASE tool repositories. These repositories (also referred to in different products as corporate data dictionaries, knowledgebases and central encyclopaedias) will be the glue that will enable enterprises to achieve full integration across the three different dimensions of integration discussed above. The first step towards achieving an integrated environment is to acknowledge the need to adopt a 'top-down' approach and to develop an enterprise model which has all of its component objects captured in a repository software tool.

Some approaches to enterprise modelling suggest that certain entities are 'persistent' and that certain elementary processes are 'ubiquitous'. Therefore, regardless of the organisational structure or changes in strategy there will always be 'products', 'customers' and 'suppliers' as well as functions carrying out 'financial', 'marketing' and 'production' activities. The assumption is that these activities have a consistent internal logic which is similar across enterprises and can be reduced to their constituent components. However, it is ultimately not a worthwhile endeavour in the opinion of this author. For to arrive at an organisation-independent model of the enterprise assumes that the modeller has the freedom to inject generic, subject area models into the metamodel and this is likely to be so different from the real enterprise that the exercise will have had little or no practical value. However, it may bear some consideration in particular circumstances such as a green-field site or where a courageous business leadership is embarking on a radical redesign of the business. In addition, it is almost always the case that the actual exercise of constructing the enterprise model with the business areas precipitates insights into the business processes in a manner that leads to some redesign. In these cases the business may benefit from comparing its own processes (which are often unduly complex) with a more elegant, generic alternative.

The main goal of the enterprise modelling endeavour is to capture a map of the business which is independent of current implementations and which will be reasonably resistant to change. This enterprise map can be constructed in two ways – it can start by taking an overall systems and data architecture or it can build up business maps from the many functional areas in a business and then integrate them. The former approach is preferable, but the latter will probably be necessary in most large organisations. Creating this high-level architecture does not in itself create any new information systems. The purpose of the architecture is to allow the enterprise to envision a target enterprise architecture which enables the enterprise, through the steady evolution and transformation of its information systems, to achieve over time. The annual output of the enterprise model is a rolling five year strategic plan which identifies the actions which are required to move the organisation and the information systems through the necessary changes.

The main aim of the strategic plan is the 'integration' of the business. Most organisations will have evolved islands of automation which give rise to a number of problems in integrating both corporate processes and corporate data. The data warehouse is, in essence, a short cut to delivering the integrated data, but it is only through the development of a target enterprise model towards which the enterprise must migrate its information systems that an integration of corporate business processes can take place.

ENTERPRISE MODELLING ROLES AND RESPONSIBILITIES

Because of the nature of enterprise modelling it will be necessary to approach the project in a manner which is participative and which is sensitive to the fears and concerns of different subject areas in the enterprise. This is best achieved by first collecting data from available sources and through standard interviews. The real task will be to reconcile the information and to attempt to locate the inputs from different parts of the organisation within an integrated framework.

Focusing Sessions

Focusing sessions will be used to validate information which has been gathered during the early stages of the requirements definition stage of the enterprise modelling project. This is a key activity because it is here that the high-level design of the data warehouse will be established and where the informating applications will be specified and prioritised.

From a political perspective it is here that the direction of the project will be determined and therefore the success of the focusing sessions will be of paramount importance (a) in identifying where the data warehouse can play a part in meeting the needs of key executives and (b) in preparing the high-level business case for proceeding with the project.

A focusing session will have different players performing different roles in the workshop. The following role definitions are provided as a guide .

The Facilitator
This is the key role and the facilitator will have overall responsibility for the design, conduct and success of the workshop. The facilitator will guide the workshop, will ensure that any principles or guidelines for the workshop are followed, will maintain a focus on the deliverable of the workshop, will highlight issues which arise, will resolve conflicts which occur and will regularly feed back information to the workshop for validation. Serious consideration should be given to appointing a trained external facilitator who is untainted by corporate politics and who is not subject to restrictions of rank or position. Provided that the workshop objectives and deliverables are clearly defined, then the facilitator need have no specialist or technical knowledge concerning the endeavour of the enterprise or any subject area in the enterprise.

There is a separate role which belongs to the facilitation process which is that of the recorder. This is probably the best role to award to the project manager since it allows the project manager to capture the information which is required without being seen to actively participate in or lead the workshop. The project manager should not, in any way, be associated with the outputs of the workshop since it will provide the project with a tangible point of reference which has been provided by the project clients. The job of the recorder is to minute the progress of the workshop, identify any issues/action points arising and to record the deliverable.

The Participants
The participants should be selected on the basis that they are the key strategic and operational decision makers in the enterprise. It may be necessary to assuage local sensitivities by having more workshops than are absolutely necessary. This is always a difficult judgement but care should be taken not to jeopardise the quality of the deliverable which is required by having passengers in a 'live' workshop. It is much more attractive, if it can be achieved without undue attention, to have additional workshops to satisfy this need. This is not to suggest that no useful material will come from such a workshop, but if the participants are not active decision makers in the area, then their views will be largely academic. For the purposes of selecting participants it may be useful to categorise candidate participants under the following headings :

- Strategic Responsibility Holder (for making decisions impacting corporate strategy) – normally a senior executive.
- Operational Responsibility Holder (for making decisions of a purely operational nature) – normally a functional manager.
- Strategic Specialist Expert (expert in some aspect of strategy) – normally a professional economist, statistician, market analyst etc.

- Operational Specialist Expert (expert in some specialist aspect of an operational process) – normally a supervisor, machine operator, administrative official etc.

These distinctions are important since there are at least these four quadrants in the decision making model. For example, it not wise to mix strategic and operational management since the two are rarely perfectly in synch and it will be likely to lead to disputes. This may be particularly so in an organisation with a decentralised executive structure headed by senior managers with an operational mission and with a centralised policy making function also manned by senior executives. It will be the task of the facilitator to build the skeleton of a bridge between these functions before putting them both into the same workshop. Likewise, it is unwise to put generalist managers who have unspecific high-level needs for information into a workshop with specialist experts who will have very specific and well-informed requirements as the latter are likely to irritate the former. In all cases it is a bad policy to mix senior managers with their subordinates since the junior partners are not likely to participate at all.

Managing Conflict
Despite the best efforts of the facilitator to carefully plan and conduct the workshops there will inevitably be some degree of disagreement. Bear in mind that the task of constructing the strategy model is straying well outside of the traditional remit of the IT function and that the development of a corporate strategy model is one of the most challenging tasks of management science. It will not be the function of the data warehouse sponsor or project manager to develop and identify appropriate corporate strategies! The task is to capture the strategies which exist in the corporation and hope that these are sufficiently coherent to use as the foundations of a corporate decision support system. Therefore there is a clear limit to where the strategy model can be brought. Not to have a strategy model at all is to build the data warehouse on shifting sands, and to await a fully coherent integrated corporate model is likely to postpone the project for ever. In addition there will be the problem that the business will say, with some justification, that the data warehouse will be the agent of a coherent strategy and that the initial prototype should proceed on the basis of minimalist knowledge of what supporting applications to construct. This runs the risk that the project will stall and be seen not to deliver anything significant and be abandoned before it has proved its worth. A clear judgement must be made at the outset of the project how much uncertainty to tolerate in the strategy model.

Outputs from the Workshops
There are three valid workshop deliverables which may be determined in advance of the workshop and which are described in this section.
(1) *Validation of strategic and operational views.*
In the first instance, hold separate workshops for the different management

levels in different functions in the enterprise. The essential task of reconciling the inputs and outputs of a group of senior executives and their subordinates in their own department and with their colleagues in another department is a secondary task which can only commence once the scale of the discrepancies is evident. The objective of this deliverable is to agree and provide a prioritised list of the key information needs of the participants.

(2)   *Consolidation of subject area views*

In the second instance, hold joint workshops for representatives of senior and operational management in the individual subject areas in order to eliminate the discrepancies which will exist in the missions and goals (and by extension, in the information requirements) of the different layers in the hierarchy. The objective here is to reconcile and relate the strategic and operational information needs of the workshop participants and to argee a prioritised list of information needs for the specific subject area.

(3)   *Consolidation of enterprise view*

Finally, the project must attempt to bring together representatives from different subject areas in order to consolidate the information needs of decision-makers who require information which is 'owned' by another subject area (or by a number of different subject areas). The objective here is to reconcile and relate the key information needs of the different subject areas and to agree a prioritised list of the high-level enterprise-wide information needs, each of which is related to a named elementary business process. There now exists, without the risk of duplication of effort, the basis for identifying the applications which can be built.

ENTERPRISE MODELLING ANALYSIS TECHNIQUES

Certain commonly occurring techniques will typically be used in order to construct a valid and comprehensive enterprise model. In particular, the following techniques are likely to be encountered by those who will be engaged in this endeavour and a brief overview description of the purpose and function of these techniques are provided here.

1. Entity Identification

Purpose: An 'entity' is a description of the primary tangible objects which occur in an enterprise.

Description: Entities are the main building blocks of the data warehouse and may be identified by nouns (things) which occur in the enterprise. It will be possible to record certain facts (called attributes) concerning an entity. Therefore an entity called EMPLOYEE will have a list of attributes which may include

Name, Address, Grade, Age etc. This is the basic raw material of a decision support system.

Example: Typical high-level entities which may occur in an enterprise are CUSTOMER, ORDER, INVOICE, EMPLOYEE etc.

Note: A high degree of difficulty is likely to be encountered in the area of entity identification and reconciliation. Many entities on different systems will describe the same object differently *(synonyms)* so that the same entity may appear as CUSTOMER, PROSPECT, PURCHASER, SUBSCRIBER on different information systems. In each case the entity may or may not have the same list of attributes. Only if you are very lucky will the attributes record the same data about the entity. You will also be likely to encounter *homonyms* – this is where a single name is used to describe different entities. An example of an homonym is where an entity called ORDER means something different on an accounts payable system (where it means 'purchase order') than it means on a sales system (where it means 'service order') than it means on a production system (where it means 'works order'). Obviously such anomalies would not have occurred where an organisation had an enterprise model in place. The enterprise will be presented with a valuable opportunity to use the data warehouse as a platform for the new enterprise model rather than attempting to cobble together new definitions of old entities in a transient environment because this is likely to lead to the data warehouse exacerbating the problem by multiplying the definitions of entities in an ad hoc fashion.

2. Entity Relationship Diagramming

Purpose: To identify the (high-level) entities which occur in an enterprise and to define the relationships which exist between the entities. The enterprise data model will provide a preliminary understanding of the enterprise in terms of the high-level data that is generated by the business and this may be broken down into a number of non-overlapping data models produced at a greater level of detail for lower-level functions/subject areas.

Description: This is perhaps the most important element of the enterprise model from the point of view of the design of the data warehouse. Here is where the data which occurs in the enterprise (and the data that does not occur in the enterprise but is required) is described. Every entity (a tangible object) which the decision maker needs to know about is described here and the relationships between the various entities identify the processes where that entity is used and therefore is a process which may be optimised through a greater knowledge of the behaviour of the entity data.

Example: A CUSTOMER (first high-level entity) PLACES (identifies relationship) ORDER (second high level entity). Typically an enterprise entity relationship diagram would contain about 50 *high-level* entities about which the enterprise would need to know a great deal in order to develop strategic planning and a typical enterprise would have many hundreds of entities in total which would be clustered in many functions/subject areas about which the operational management of the enterprise would need to have a knowledge of the behaviour of the data.

3. Elementary Process Identification

Purpose: To identify and describe the key high-level processes in the enterprise.

Description: Elementary processes are the basic logical units of work in the enterprise and each elementary process may possess many lower-level processes. Every business process should occur in response to an event. It will not be absolutely uncommon to find processes in an enterprise which occur without any stimulus. It is very likely that the enterprise should consider ceasing this process or at least consider it a candidate for business process redesign. An elementary process is normally described in terms of a business transaction and most processes will be computerised on online systems. These processes will create the data which will form the source data for the warehouse.

Example: An elementary process is normally described in terms of process properties which will normally include a process name, a process definition, an activating event, a location in the organisation and the frequency of the process.

4. Entity Life Cycle Analysis

Purpose: This technique is used to associate the data model and the process model in a particular business area and to validate the completeness and consistency of both.

Description: A data model comprises a number of entities each of which has relationships with other entities in the model. Each of these entities has a lifecycle. This lifecycle begins when an occurrence of the entity is 'created' and the lifecycle ends with the deletion of the entity. The entity may be changed by an elementary process which impacts on that entity. Therefore a diagram outlining the lifecycle of an entity is presented as a record of the transition of the entity from one state to another and allows the analyst to observe all of the business processes that are dependent on the entity.

Example: An entity called ORDER can be impacted by a number of elementary processes which can change the state of the entity from being PLACED to being CONFIRMED to being CANCELLED to being RE-ORDERED etc.

5. Event Analysis

Purpose: This technique is used to describe events which are clustered around interdependent processes in a manner which allows the analyst to sub-divide the enterprise into lower-level functions or subject areas.

Description: Event analysis is one of the most common techniques used to discover and describe the elementary processes which occur in an enterprise. Therefore, it is reasonable to say that a high-level event must trigger an

elementary process in the enterprise. Events must be described and analysed at an atomic level in the enterprise and are sometimes described as 'discrete events'.
Example: CUSTOMER PLACES ORDER is a discrete high-level event which activates at least one elementary process which, in turn, activates other events and processes.

6. Association Diagramming

Purpose: To capture for analysis the association which exists between two objects resident in the enterprise model.
Description: Normally presented in a matrix format with the associations between the two objects identified. The most common and valuable association matrix analysed during enterprise modelling is the *elementary process* to *data entity* matrix which identified what processes interact with what data in the enterprise.
Example: In a real example there would be an entity on one axis, say CUSTOMER, which would act on or be acted on by a number of processes on the other axis – the entity CUSTOMER would be updated by the process CLOSE ACCOUNT.

7. Critical Success Factor Analysis

Purpose: To identify at a high level what conditions must obtain in order for the enterprise to function effectively in the market.
Description: Critical Success Factors (CSFs) are always a useful tool to use as a base reference point in any important information systems project because decisions on the nature of the system or the priority of the components of the system can be assessed by reference to the degree that they support the stated corporate (or functional) CSFs. It is also a useful way of ensuring that some general agreement is reached by different user constituencies at the outset of the project. CSFs should normally be presented as a prioritised list and are related to missions, goals and measurable objectives for the business which have been captured during the preliminary analysis stage of the enterprise modelling project. It is important to note that CSFs are normally defined as conditions which must exist and which the body corporate can influence the achievement of the factors identified. Where a factor is not directly controlled by the enterprise, but is of critical importance, it may be referred to as a 'critical assumption' and these may be listed separately.
Example: An example of a critical success factor for a marketing division may be, 'that the enterprise will have a thorough understanding of customer behaviour', while a critical assumption may be, 'that the enterprise will not be subject to substantial currency fluctuations'.

8. SWOT Analysis

Purpose: To identify and present the strengths, weaknesses, threats and opportunities associated with a course of action.

Description: In an enterprise model this technique is commonly used to analyse architectural or application options. Essentially, SWOT analysis is a simple analytic tool to ease decision making which assists in identifying the impacts of a particular decision.

Example: When a project has reached a decision point, such as deciding the first application to be provided from the data warehouse, there will be many competing concerns like the business benefit of making a specific application available (strength), the difficulty in accessing the source data (weakness), the lack of clarity of the user requirements (threat) and the ability to use the same data sets to provide another application easily (opportunity).

9. Information Needs Analysis

Purpose: To provide a guide at a strategic level and at an operational level what are the key information needs of the key decision makers.

Description: Normally strategic information is needed for planning and policy making while operational information is required for monitoring and controlling. It will be important when considering the information needs of decision makers to bear in mind that they are going to be conditioned by their knowledge of what actually exists and therefore it will be important to try to get them to 'think out of the box' and it will be equally important to bear in mind that the results will only be a guide to the information requirements, particularly in respect of the strategic information needs. It will be necessary during this analysis to identify key characteristics of the information which will influence the database design at a later stage such as frequency, coverage, level of detail etc.

Example: A strategic decision maker may wish to know biannually 'The variation in profitability of a certain product in a particular market segment over a number of years', while it may be an operation information need of another decision maker to know every week 'How many units of the product were sold to that segment last week'.

10. Current Systems Evaluation

Purpose: To provide a basis for measuring the distance from the current actually existing architecture to the conceptual model of the enterprise which has been constructed.

Description : This is a kind of 'clash analysis' where the ideal model is clashed against the actual applications and the difference between the two represents the amount of effort required to deliver the additional functionality that the business requires.

The evaluation of existing systems is an analysis in three stages. In the first stage, which is technically oriented, the objective is to identify and audit the existing systems where each application is analysed under headings such as operating system platform, file structure, data communications protocols, database product and type, application environment (programming language), number of lines of code, number of function points and other architectural characteristics. In the second stage the relevant headings are user oriented and include concerns such as security, data ownership, business alignment, backlog of system enhancements, and interaction with other systems. In the final stage some judgements must be made concerning the degree of satisfaction with the system. With regard to the requirement of the business for information, this final stage should have particular regard to evaluating the accuracy, comprehensiveness, reliability, timeliness and the ease of access to data in the existing systems.

Example : A stage three analysis would identify the information needs of an enterprise and the degree to which they support the critical success factors of the business and will then indicate the degree to which this need is satisfied by the different systems which might reasonably be expected to satisfy this need.

Note: This analysis will provide some key inputs to the justification of the business case for the data warehouse since this technique will have demonstrated the ability of the existing portfolio of information systems to meet the demands of the business for information to support decision making.

Chapter 6
Mass Customisation of Products and Services: The Future Trend

THE TRANSITION FROM MASS PRODUCTION

Mass production was, and is, the dominant form of industrial production. It came into being for reasons which had become apparent in the manufacturing process in the early twentieth century. Prior to mass production each product was individually crafted by highly skilled specialist workers. The manufacture of the Model T Ford became the modern icon of mass production and central to the philosophy of Henry Ford was that products were produced in a standard uniform fashion. The process of mass production was refined according to the principles of the noted management scientist, Frederick Taylor, who designed work in a manner which consciously replaced craftsmen with untrained operatives. Despite a good deal of evidence which recommends the re-integration of work, most organisations are still organised in separate functional streams according to Taylorist principles with task demarcation at the level of workers and decision demarcation at the managerial level.

The alienation of the customer in a system of mass production is evident to anyone who has commented on the sameness of consumer products and the delight experienced in receiving of a handwritten letter in a modern world of junk mail, stylesheets, and other cynical ploys such as the marketing letter that says 'Dear Mr Smith' but has the same text for hundreds of thousands of others. These cynical attempts at personalisation actually represent the antithesis of customisation. Personalisation occurs only at the customer interface; behind that smiling exterior exists the old mass production factory grinding on as it has done for decades. Customisation, on the other hand, penetrates the entire enterprise which is structured in such a fashion which can adapt to different customer requirements. The personalisation of a tee-shirt or tailormade clothes or even the famous cabbage patch doll provide uniqueness, but it is a uniqueness embedded in the product itself. The value of a personalised product is not that it can be invented or re-invented by its owner, but that it is exclusive to its owner.

Customisation, on the other hand, is attempting a much more substantial feat – it is assisting the customer to select the optimum product for his or her needs and then providing that product and going on to adjust that product as the needs of the customer change. The product *per se* may not be personalised in any way. For example, there is no way that telephone service can be made more exclusive. After all, dial tone is dial tone. The customisation will reside in the manner in which the product is delivered. Discounting schemes, call plans and value added services (call forwarding, call waiting etc.) are the means of customisation, not the product itself. In the book *Future Perfect* Stan Davis declares 'standardise the commodity and customise the service that surrounds it'. [18]

How many consumers of bank services have received a computer-generated letter that informs them that they are two pounds overdrawn on their current account because the computer is programmed to issue this format to everybody including those who make scheduled weekly deposits of one thousand pounds? How many consumers of utility services have gone on an extended holiday abroad and found all the services cut off when they returned, even though they had paid their utility bills assiduously for decades? These are the events which infuriate customers. Yet all of these organisations had all of the data that they needed to know these things. In all of their computers they have amassed all of this data and yet they can draw no useful conclusions about the behaviour of their customers.

Genuine mass customisation is an attempt to establish a real and informed dialogue with the customer and to demonstrate that the organisation has a knowledge of the behaviour of that customer over time. The present dynamic of a changing market along with technological drivers have combined to evolve the concept of mass customisation. There is compelling evidence that companies which manage to transform their production and delivery processes to the new model of mass customisation will enjoy significant competitive advantage in the marketplace. Central to the concept of mass customisation is the micro-segmentation of markets down to fine levels of granularity in order to customise the product offerings to the multiple segments. Of course this will not occur in a single event. The process will commence with segmentation at a high level and will progressively expand until the final objective of mass customisation has been achieved – a market segment of *one* customer! The progression from mass market through niche markets to segmented markets and finally to the customised marketplace is illustrated in Figure 7.

MARKET SEGMENTATION

The traditional way in which markets have been segmented has been on the basis of objective externally observed phenomena and has been confined largely to demographic data. The main impetus behind target marketing arose because of the identification of socio-economic groups by newspapers. Originally there were six groupings – A, B, C1, C2, D and E – determined by reference to the occupation of the head of household. Over time the C1 group (skilled manual) and the C2 group (supervisory/clerical) merged in terms of buying patterns and the market is now frequently reduced to three segments of roughly equivalent size – ABC1, C2 and DE. It has been observed (somewhat rudely) that A/Bs had taste and money, C1s taste but no money, C2s money but no taste and D/E's no taste and no money. [19]

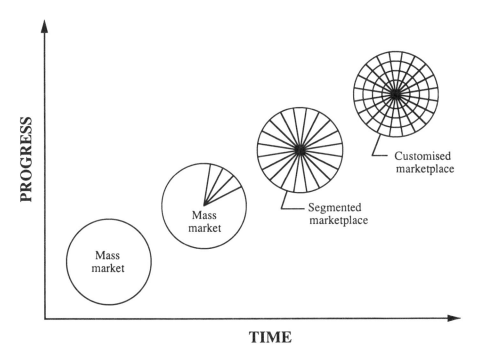

TIME

Figure 7   From mass to customised market.

Thus a producer of a product can make some assumptions about a customer who was categories as A2 (professional person) that would differentiate this customer from a C1 customer (clerical/supervisory). This technique is said to have been originally devised by a British army recruiting sergeant as a means of establishing the social backgrounds of recruits during the First World War and it has not matured in sophistication since then. As a general system of classifying customers or prospective customers it is notoriously deficient and even in the United Kingdom the class distinctions upon which the definitions were based have eroded considerably in recent decades. It is a common tendency in the buying patterns of consumers with relatively modest disposable income to indulge in at least one consumer habit which would traditionally have been associated with a different group. In addition it is the case that all social classes purchase the same commodity products (e.g. petrol) albeit in different quantities.

A number of alternative methods of customer segmentation have been based on neighbourhood classifications, for instance, the principle of postcode analysis. One of these is ACORN (A Classification of Residential Neighbourhoods) which is used by some enterprises in the United Kingdom as a basis for segmentation. This method provides a basis, albeit crude, for determining the income levels of prospective customers.

The emerging basis for determining the classifications of customers will be a good deal more intangible and will focus on the behaviour patterns of the customer. Therefore, a customer may be observed to be compulsive (or conservative) in his/her consumption habits; may have established consumption trends based on special interests (e.g. gardening, motoring); may have displayed a particular pattern of annual income and expenditure; may have displayed a seasonal pattern of consumption; may have demonstrated a particular sequence of product consumption. Or groups of customers may have identified a pattern of consumption which allows a new product to be designed around their needs. All of these judgements about the customer are now derived from the actual behaviour of the customer rather than assumptions about how people in particular social categories might be expected to behave. The source of determining customer behaviour patterns lies in integrating and observing data patterns. Current information systems are not designed to perform this function. The data warehouse is designed to specifically provide the information required for mass customisation.

This change in the manner in which enterprises must regard the new marketplace is encapsulated in the following passage by Stan Davis.

We are familiar with allocating tangible resources (labour, capital, equipment) to create tangible products (food, cars, housing) and tangible services (restaurants, telephones) for tangible market segments (middleclass male professional, teenage suburban athlete).

By comparison, we are less practiced in allocating intangible resources (mind, time, information) to create intangible products (software, advertisements, investments) and intangible services (personal shoppers, health, education) for intangible market segments (conservatives, compulsives', swingers). [20]

All of the data which can be combined to provide an integrated profile of the customer is shown in Figure 8.

Figure 8: A multi dimensional customer profile.

CUSTOMISATION AND DATA

From an organisational point of view customisation will precipitate a shift from disaggregating to re-aggregating the production process. The knowledgeworker will be the craftsman of the late twentieth century and the primary skill that will define the knowledgeworker will be the ability to manipulate and analyse data patterns and to advocate strategic directions on the basis of that analysis.

A mass production process requires a stable environment and generates a regular demand for large quantities of *internal control* data (financial reports, production reports etc.). The key deficiency in mass production has been its inability to quickly re-focus the goals and resources of the production process. The only response of a mass production organisation to adverse trading conditions is to retrench, cut costs and hope to weather the storm.

On the other hand the mass customisation organisation is more concerned with obtaining *external customer data* (customer behaviour, market movement etc.). The conditioned response of a mass customisation organisation to adversity in the market is to engage in a perpetual war of manoeuvre which invents, re-invents and customises its products and services in an effort to constantly mirror (and anticipate) changes in the external environment. The mass production abhors turbulence in the market while the mass customisation creates turbulence.

One of the most visible example of mass customisation in practice can be observed in the competitive cauldron of US telecommunications suppliers. Customers are now offered a dazzling array of alternative 'call-plans' which may be selected on the basis of choosing the cheapest plan which can accommodate the likely pattern of telephone calls which a customer may make. For example, if a telephone customer makes a lot of telephone calls internationally or only makes local calls, the services and discounts which they may opt for will be different. In this particular example the products which they receive (i.e. dial tone) will not actually be different – the element that is customised is the pricing package.

This example is also interesting in a second respect. Telephone companies, like many utilities, build an infrastructure designed to deal with the peak load on the system. Therefore telephone networks and electricity generating facilities tend to be highly inefficient from an investment point of view because they are virtually idle during the night and over weekends. Part of the customised pricing package is designed not only to offer attractive discounts to particular segments of the market but also to enhance the utilisation of the network by encouraging customers with particular traffic patterns to transfer their consumption to the off-peak period when there is no additional cost involved in switching the calls thereby flattening the variations in production output. In this regard it can be claimed that by carefully manipulating the uncertainty which obtains in the external environment a supplier can build stability into the internal production process. Thus, from sophisticated analysis of the complex usage patterns the telecommunications service provider can construct a classic win–win situation for producer *and* consumer. Now that data pattern analysis engines are being used by most of the competing telecommunications providers in the US, the main focus has shifted to assessing the impact of competitors 'call-plans' and in responding with newly designed plans which are designed to nullify the competing alternative. In this highly competitive arena the characteristic which is increasingly evident in the data warehouse implementations is the increasingly granular (i.e detailed) nature of the data being stored in the systems.

A third lesson which may be gleaned from this example is that suppliers can engage in clever customer entrapment strategies when it comes to offering customised services. Take a customer who typically would receive telephone service from one supplier, cellular service from another, a paging/answering service from another etc. A customised service for this customer is likely to be directed at designing a package which is attractive to the customer on the basis of their typical behaviour patterns but which integrates the services in a manner which locks the customer into a single vendor contract.

A key element of the concept of customisation is the separation of the product and process lifecyles. The process lifecycle becomes the primary element in the production process and it will have the capability of plugging multiple products or variations into the process. This will bring some stability to the production process but it is likely that, in general, this kind of model will lead to substantial and regular redesign of business processes. Of course, the incremental product innovation which will accrue from the mass customisation system will lead to the fragmentation of the market into multiple niches, but the mass customisation business can be exposed to fundamental product innovations which will reverse the fragmentation trend and will lead to the dominance of products which enjoy some single proprietary advantage. But such events will in turn be overtaken as the innovation is replicated and in turn customised and fragmented as the market awaits the next fundamental innovation.

In the consumer product market the automobile industry is a good example of mass customisation in action. For some time now motor manufacturers such as Volvo have been offering customers (in limited markets) choice combinations as to colour, trim, facilities and extras in advance of the purchase. Regarded from a purely mathematical perspective it is instructive to note that a manufacturer of a product who allows a customer to select six different attributes from a list of 36 possible attributes faces 2 million different combinations of six! The National Bicycle Industrial Company in Kobubu, Japan, markets made-to-measure bicycles. They are delivered within two weeks of the order being placed and the company offers 11 232 862 combinations of variation at prices only 10% higher than standard adjustable bicycles. [21] Henry Ford would have been aghast. Volvo has been at the forefront in rolling back mass production. At its assembly plant at Uddevalla in south-west Sweden, cars are being assembled by teams in a stationary position – not in a moving line – without supervisors or foremen. Part of the benefits are experienced in higher satisfaction and lower rates of absenteeism by the workers. But the real benefits will be realised in the marketplace because of the ability of the production process to produce unique products at no extra cost. Increasingly we see newspapers customising their editions on a regional basis. How long will it be before they begin to customise the news?

The dilemma of adapting the manufacturing/service-delivery process to deal with the complexity of producing 2 million different variables is immense and throws up one of the main dilemmas of utilising data warehouse technology. What if the data warehouse can determine the market requirement for customisation and the operational systems (manufacturing, billing etc.) cannot deliver the customisation ? Then the entire endeavour begins to look academic. This is why the assessment of the value of the data warehouse to the business must be seen in the context not only of what the data will reveal but also of how the enterprise will benefit from the revelation.

Customisation is made possible by flexible manufacturing, just as segmentation is made possible by information. Both information and flexible manufacturing are enabled by technology. Technology first creates the conditions for change – the business must then adapt to exploit the opportunity.

THE BENEFITS OF CUSTOMISATION

A general overview of the benefits of a customisation culture may be presented in terms of the two partners in the process. These are the customer and the organisation.

The Customer

The main goals of the marketing effort associated with customisation will be customer retention and customer satisfaction. The 'surprise and delight' nature of customised products and services will significantly enhance the ability of the business to gain new customers and retain existing ones. These goals will be achieved by establishing a personal relationship with the customer by demonstrating a knowledge of the customer's behaviour and by designing products which suit that behaviour. This will be especially important for customers who purchase different products and services from an enterprise and who wish to receive credit for their full value to the enterprise. This will involve integrating the data about that customer which is scattered throughout the enterprise. The customisation of services will also tap latent demand among customers to purchase services which would not otherwise be on offer. In addition, the customer will enjoy a comfort factor if the service which has been purchased can be altered and changed.

The Organisation

The primary benefit to the organisation is the external focus of the customer and the requirements of the customer. The customisation of services will require constant innovation and the incentive to innovate in order to meet customer requirements is a useful alternative to the traditional incentive to innovate which was based on the activity of the competitor. This benefit of achieving an external focus in the absence of a competitor would also provide a useful mechanism for organisational stimulation in monopoly organisations.

CONCLUSION

The customisation of the market represents a profound change in the manner in which industrial production occurs and will dramatically accelerate the twin trends which are already occurring – the demand for greater market intelligence and the re-assessment of business processes. If mass customisation is the driver of industrial innovation and if the networked organisation is the vehicle of industrial production, then the data warehouse will be a key component of the enabling technology.

These three phenomena have emerged organically from three different fields of endeavour – from marketing science, computer science and organisational theory. It will be the synergy between these three components which will serve to provide a map of future strategic directions for a successful commercial culture.

Chapter 7

Aligning the Data Warehouse with Organisational Culture: a Key Concern

One of the greatest challenges to be encountered by the sponsor of any major initiative in an enterprise is to correctly align the project with the organisational culture in a way that does not threaten the integrity of that project. Even before this challenge is faced the organisation itself must agree and construct a sponsorship model for the project. The roots of failure of pan-corporate projects are usually to be found in the 'political' context of the sponsorship/ownership model of the system being introduced and this specific element of the project is explored in more detail in the next chapter. The problem of alignment becomes particularly acute in the data warehouse project because the co-operation is required of many departmental managers in assembling functional data into an integrated corporate whole, and the very notion of a corporate view of the truth rather than a controlled functional version of the truth may be perceived as threatening by some managers in the defensive 'blame and recrimination' cultures which are prevalent in many organisations.

In addition the data warehouse (or, more properly, the knowledge gained from the data warehouse) is likely to precipitate a good deal of redesign of existing business processes and the mechanism for dealing with these changes should be anticipated and decided at an early stage in the project. For example the patterns of customer behaviour exhibited by the patterns of data in the data warehouse may precipitate demands in the business for changes in product design or in the service delivery process. It will be quite common for data warehouse applications to function as event alerters which raise flags in the operational systems when a threat or opportunity condition is identified through an analysis of the data. In this way strategy formulation becomes a dynamic activity which seeks to impact on the business processes in real time.

Finally, there is likely to be some resistance from the information system providers in the organisation because the data warehouse represents a different model for the development of a corporate decision support capability and it may take time for many software engineers to come to terms with the model. It will be just as important to enjoy the goodwill of all the software engineers in the IT department as it is to enjoy the goodwill of the functional managers for precisely the same reason – the data being integrated in the warehouse must be extracted from all of the existing corporate systems, ideally by the personnel responsible for the care and maintenance of those systems. For many software engineers trained in the conventional techniques of systems design will initially baulk at some features of the data warehouse and will point to data duplication, data redundancy, lack of enterprise architectures and lack of specification rigour as reasons not to proceed with the project. Ultimately the software engineering cadre generally will have to face two essential truths. One is that there is an unavoidable performance obstacle to running decision support programs concurrent with online access for transaction users and that this technological obstacle will continue to exist for at least the next decade. Secondly, information systems designers have now amassed a sufficient store of empirical evidence to suggest that users' failure to define their requirements for queries is not due to any bloody-mindedness on the part of users and that the continued search for methodological rigour in this area is simply a foolish endeavour.

A HISTORY OF ORGANISATIONAL TRANSITION

It is useful when approaching the topic of organisational alignment to reflect on the continuum of organisational change in the course of this century. In the early decades of the century the main concern of organisational science was focused on *structure* and was driven, at that time, by the development at General Motors of the functional model of the organisation. During the inter-war years and up to the nineteen-sixties the influence of Frederick Taylor and the cult of scientific management focused organisational attention on the subject of *productivity*. During the nineteen-sixties and up to the eighties the impact of computerisation had the effect of presenting the organisation in terms of the sum total of *systems* which the organisation deployed. Organisational concern in the nineteen-eighties and the early nineties has focused on a *socio-cultural* agenda which is concerned with the full utilisation of human resources through leadership, motivation, team-work, empowerment and participation. Organisational science is now at a stage where a new departure must soon be identified and there is enough evidence to suspect that the core of this new departure will be centred on a concern with *information*.

THE ORGANISATION AND DECISION MAKING

In what is possibly the seminal work on the subject of the relationship between decision making and organisational design H. A. Simon [22] divides the decision making process into three phases. The first phase, which Simon called the *intelligence* activity, is concerned with gathering data. The second phase, which is called the *design* activity, is concerned with modelling and analysing the different courses of action which are possible in the circumstances. And the third phase is called the *choice* activity and is simply concerned with selecting a solution. Simon correctly identified a common misconception with decision making which focuses almost entirely on the final phase – the moment of decision – while ignoring 'the whole lengthy, complex process of alerting, exploring and analysing that precedes that final moment'.

It is from Simon's distinction between *programmed* and *non-programmed* decisions that the distinction between ad hoc queries and decision support applications can be made. Simon associated programmed decision making with the middle layer of management. His definition of programmed decisions as 'repetitive' is an accurate reflection of those decisions which are amenable to being supported by decision support applications which may be built for a defined set of users and which allows them to navigate through the data within a reasonably structured environment. 'Decisions are non-programmed', according to Simon, 'to the extent that they are novel, unstructured and consequential'. This category of decision making is associated by Simon with senior management in organisations where their requirement for data would encompass the external environment as well as the internal corporate sources of data. Therefore unstructured decision making can only be supported by ad hoc queries of a wide range of data. From a decisional point of view and from a software point of view it is essential to comprehend and acknowledge that these two kinds of decision making each require a different approach from the system designer.

The complex level of decision making will require a wide expanse of data and will involve very complex ad hoc queries, but the absolute number of these kinds of queries which will need to be executed will be very limited. The intermediate level of decision making will require at least a functional expanse of data and will be supported by queries which are repetitive and can be accommodated by decision support applications accessing the data warehouse. At the lowest level are operational queries relating to routine operational decisions and these should be supported by the operational transaction systems in the enterprise and are not usually proper to a data warehouse environment at all. The distinction between the strategic level, the tactical level and the operational level of decision making is identified in Figure 9.

ORGANISATION STRUCTURE AND THE DATA WAREHOUSE

However, there is one prediction made by Simon in 1960 which is failing to survive the test of time, and that is the durability of the hierarchical structure in

Figure 9   The hierarchy of queries generated by the different layers of
management

organisations. Simon asserted that, largely because of the deployment of
computerised systems which would assist decision making, the task of
disseminating this information would only be manageable where the data could be
partitioned according to function and rank. The concept that many parts of the
organisation would require *all* of the corporate data to support their activities
seems to have been regarded by Simon as eccentric. From Simon's perspective,
and from the perspective of the era in which he was working and writing, it was
an eccentric idea. The explosion of information was foreseen (but not the
technological capability to process it), and the hierarchical organisation was seen
as the most efficient mechanism to manage this complexity. 'Hierarchical systems
require much less information transmission among their parts than do other types
of systems', declared Simon. The notion of all of the decision makers accessing all
of the corporate data implied that the volumes of data that would have to be
transmitted within the organisation would grow proportionately with the square of
its size. It was an appalling prospect. And it has come to pass.

While it perfectly reasonable for a data warehouse to be constructed in order to provide control reports in a rigid hierarchically structured organisation or even for multiple departmental data warehouses to be constructed to support decision making in diverse departments, the essential philosophy of the data warehouse is based on the concept of leveraging advantage from the *integration* of data. Inherent in this philosophy is the simple concept that through the integration a pattern will emerge that was not previously visible and that the totality of the pattern has more value to the business than the sum of the parts. The different data requirements of the different levels of management in the organisation are identified in Figure 10.

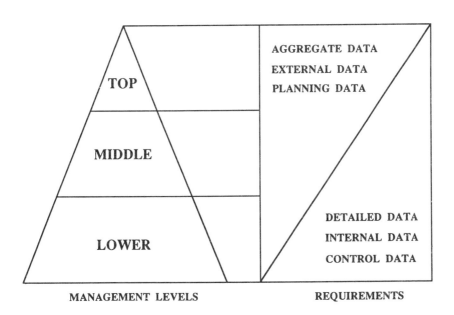

Figure 10 The requirements for data of the different managerial levels

The data warehouse, and, more importantly, the applications which access the data in the data warehouse, will have the effect of shortening the distance between *devising* candidate strategies at a senior level in an organisation and *executing* the selected strategy at an operational level. This will lead to an immediate 'flattening' of the decision making process which will have fairly radical follow-on implications for the formal organisational structure and culture. At present most corporate strategy is devised on the basis of aggregate information combined artificially from systems that are not integrated. The only meaningful basis upon which to determine key decisions in the enterprise is detailed and integrated data which can provide accurate answers and, more importantly, can provide a comprehensive guide as to the impact of the decision.

Of course, a good deal of corporate strategy is determined on an ad hoc basis and it is not that uncommon for an operational memorandum to wind its way vertically up through an organisation and to trigger an isolated (and often disastrous) decision at a strategic level.

In most organisations information of various kinds travels up through the organisation and decisions of various kinds are handed down through the layers of the organisation. This kind of structure may be identified as hierarchic, functional, or bureaucratic, or as a 'role centred' culture in that it may have some (or all) of these organisational characteristics. As a general rule this type of organisation will have a tendency to centralise the key policy making (and even key operational) decision making and will behave in a rational, highly ordered fashion and will normally have in place mature and stable business processes. In general, decisions (whether strategic or operational) tend to be devised and executed on the basis of command-and-control principles. Despite the efforts of many organisational scientists (and many well-intentioned initiatives by organisations) this organisational structure persists as the most common form of management culture which obtains in industry, commerce or the public service. The implementation of a pan-corporate decision support system can encounter specific serious difficulties in this organisational culture which require specific responses which are explored later in this chapter.

The most common alternative organisational model in business is the network model, which tends to be highly decentralised with more autonomy in the hands of local decision makers. This structure presents its own problems in the design of a system but on a much less daunting scale. The implementation of a corporate data warehouse is easily embedded in a networked or matrix structure where a 'goal-centred' culture is dominant and where functional boundaries are more blurred. This type of organisation is likely to be project-focused and will regard information like any other corporate resource at the disposal of the project.

Changes in organisational structure and management cultures are closely linked to changes in methods of production, which are in turn linked to technological innovation. In that sense it is unclear whether the data warehouse will be subordinate to the organisational structure and designed according to the characteristics of the culture resident in a given organisation or whether it will serve to undermine and ultimately to replace the organisational culture of the business. In this sense the warehouse may be seen to be a non-neutral component of the culture in an organisation.

In the command-type organisational structure many layers of the hierarchy exist for the expressed purpose of evaluating the data which is constantly in transit. Value is added to the data in circulation by a process of communication between managers and decision makers and decisions are informed by synergies between various items of data from various departments which may be assembled into a piece of usable information upon which to base a decision. Generally speaking, there is a reasonably good quality of decision making in each individual function but the speed and quality deteriorate when cross-functional data is required. Therefore the organisation may have excellent production, financial, marketing, logistics and personnel functions supported by excellent individual information systems but still produce lousy widgets and deliver them to the wrong place at the wrong time.

In an environment of incomplete information the most valuable asset a manager can have is good intuition. Many managers will have been chosen precisely because they have this attribute and have demonstrated that they can very often (but not always) predict the mood of a market. Of course, this is not rational behaviour since there is a high likelihood that the decision will be wrong, but it is nonetheless common behaviour. Arguably, it is likely to be more successful than basing all decisions on the incomplete information since this is guaranteed to produce a wrong decision.

One of the most pervasive recent developments in industrial organisation structure is the emergence of the *modular corporation* which is based on the premise that executive decision makers should focus their attention on the core activities of the enterprise only, and subcontract the non-core activities to other modules of the corporation which will generally be other independent companies. This tendency had its roots in the Japanese model of 'lean production' where two distinctive industrial sectors existed – one was the few core companies which devised and sold products into the market and the other was the many non-core companies which were subcontractors to the centre. What this means in practice is that an organisation may concentrate on design and marketing and leave the production, materials sourcing, accounting and distribution functions to other independent modules. The performance of the non-core functions may be subject to stringent standards and quality audits or open to competitive tender. Each modular block of the corporation can be removed, replaced or adapted without endangering the entire structure. The obvious flexibility of the modular model contrasts starkly with the hierarchical command structure where every function *has* the potential to endanger the entire structure because the command-and-control organism is designed to be a self-sufficient interdependent whole.

The primary benefits of concentrating on core competencies and out-sourcing the rest are psychological – it makes the corporation 'mindsized' and key decision makers can concentrate on the key issues rather than being distracted by a plethora of issues which are always urgent, but ultimately not important.

The lead in this area has been taken by the electronic and clothing companies and one of the most visible characteristics of the modular corporation is the 're-badged' product. This occurs when a company with distribution channels to a market orders a product to meet the needs of that market from another company (often a competitor) which is marketed under the name of the modular company. This phenomenon is now being reflected in the way that organisations view their relationships with each other. Traditionally an organisation had a one-dimensional relationship with another. Now that relationship is multi-dimensional – one organisation may easily be a supplier to, be supplied from, be a competitor with, be a strategic partner of, and be a joint venture partner with another corporation (or with various parts of another corporation).

But this trend is also moving out of the sectors which originally adopted it. Chrysler, the US auto manufacturer has implemented 'lean production' and now purchases almost 70% of its parts from outside contractors, (almost as much as Toyota), and increasingly suppliers are delivering pre-assembled sections rather than component-level parts.

Lean production techniques proved to be remarkably resilient in absorbing the shocks of market turbulence in the 1970s and 1980s. This 'disaggregation' of industrial organisations has fundamental implications for the design and delivery of corporate decision support capability. Increasingly the enterprise will comprise the sum total of competencies and resources which can be brought to bear on a market opportunity. Eventually the enterprise will become a 'virtual reality' comprising only two key ingredients – an *information* asset and the *skill* to exploit that asset.

When considering the relationship between organisational structure and information systems a key distinction must be made between operational (transaction) systems and dedicated decision support systems. What a transaction system is normally designed to do is to automate a business process in the workplace. Some processes are cross-functional, but most processes are still confined to a single functional area. Therefore processes like generating bills, producing the weekly payroll, printing invoices, recording stock levels etc. are concerned with a functional task that is the responsibility of an individual functional manager. Because the automated system is replacing a manual system (or an older computerised system) there is likely to be some organisational impact. This normally is taken into account by the systems analyst and business manager jointly, by making some adjustments to the business process by redesigning forms, job descriptions, sequence of activities, etc. But, because the business process is confined within functional boundaries, the organisational changes will also be confined to the immediate habitat of the business process and the process itself is a clearly visible measurable phenomenon. And finally, the changes which will impact on the process will affect relatively low-level operatives who are tasked with carrying out the process.

A decision support project on the scale of a data warehouse is likely to have the potential for a more traumatic impact on the delicate equilibrium of an organisational culture. The deployment of a fully functional data warehouse with the capability to automate a good deal of the decision making process, if indeed it can be described at this time as a process, will present a direct threat to the pillars of the organisational structure which rise through the layers of the conventional organisation. It has the potential to fundamentally disrupt the existing structure. Unlike the impact on a business transaction process the corporate decision support system will traverse functional boundaries, will transform a process which is ill-defined and nebulous and will impact on the most senior managers in the corporation. For that reason the corporate data warehouse will be, for most enterprises, a delicate endeavour.

THE IMPACT OF THE DATA WAREHOUSE

At the end of this section the question must be posed, 'Is a corporate data warehouse organisationally neutral?' I have described at a fairly high level the design implications of different organisational structures and cultures and this is designed to provide the system designer and sponsor with a template to manage the risk inherent in the project and to optimise the design by providing a correct alignment. However, the question is still valid and deserves some exploration. It is the view of this author, having studied success and failure stories in the short history of building the data warehouse that a certain organic link exists between the data warehouse and a goal oriented open culture. The primary reason why this is the case is that a role oriented hierarchical functional structure will always seek, by its very nature, to define the decision support requirements of different levels in different functions on the basis of *control data* which is required in the administration process. If this is, in fact, the narrow and structured access to the data warehouse then it will be very difficult for the system designer to answer the question, 'Why not build the reporting requirements into the online transaction processing systems?' After all, the entire *raison d'etre* for the data warehouse is to integrate data, to transform data and to use it to navigate the external environment, not the internal environment.

Notwithstanding that, many hierarchical corporations will build very successful data warehouses because the current systems do not satisfy the need for control reports. But the data warehouse will have the potential to be a subversive agent in this kind of environment because once the potential exists for open access to integrated pictures then decision makers will agitate to eat the forbidden fruit!

In the past the power of computers was brought to bear on the challenge of reducing process cycle times. Now attention is turning to the challenge of shortening the decision cycle and is targeted squarely on improving the productivity of knowledgeworkers. The information age organisation will shed many of these managers and the organisational structure will ultimately be reduced to the only necessary elemental decision processes which are required – strategic decisions makers and expert operational decision makers – and very little else in between. For the data warehouse designer the achievement of a congruent synchrony between the strategic and operational perspectives of data will present one of the central design challenges of the project. Success in this endeavour will require the designer to turn a deaf ear to the plaintive pleas of middle managers to reproduce the complex and dysfunctional web of relationships required to sanction decisions in the pre-information environment and proceed to deliver the means of obliterating the old world. Just as traditional transaction systems eliminated the need for many manual processes the corporate decision support systems will eliminate the need for many decision and whole layers of management will, over time, be 'de-materialised'.

In summarising the issues which impact on organisational alignment the characteristics of (internally focused) control cultures and (externally focused) market led-cultures are compared. The attributes of a data warehouse which would reside in either of these organisational environments is also sketched out. Needless to say, most organisations share some of the characteristics of the two cultures, or are in transition from one culture to the other or may have corporate sub-cultures which exhibit contrary characteristics. But most enterprises, while defying neat compartmentalisation, will have a dominant culture which will fall into one or other category.

Control Culture
The characteristics of a control culture are set out as follows :

(1) Control organisations are internally focussed.
Informating applications are likely to be financial, statistical, technical with a strong emphasis on measuring the performance of the organisation against internally generated targets.
(2) Control organisations are hierarchical.
Informating applications will have many interfaces for the needs of different management levels with access privileges associated with these needs.
(3) Control organisations tend to be rigidly functional.
Informating applications will have strict boundaries with the data in the data warehouse functionally partitioned.
(4) Control organisations are heavily centralised.
The data warehouse is likely to conform to an information factory with a tendency for users not to have direct access and for reports to be output at a central location and distributed to managers according to defined requirements and intervals.
(5)Control organisations will tend to view information as a weapon.
The data warehouse may be heavily 'politicised' with many applications fragmented and independently specified.
(6) Control organisations have defined and mature processes for progressing decisions.
Informating applications are likely to be rigourously specified and will remain durable over a long period of time.

(7) Control organisations comprise many interdependent parts.
Informating applications which identify changes which should occur in operational systems in order to pursue a market opportunity may not always be acted on because of a high level of process flexibility failure.

Market-led Culture

(1) Market-led organisations are externally focused.
Informating applications are likely to be located in the marketing function and are likely to incorporate significant volumes of external data.
(2)Market-led organisations tend to have flat structures.
Informating applications will have a small number of interfaces and decision making will be likely to be devolved to a highly empowered   front   line management cadre.
(3) Market-led organisations are organised around customers.
Informating applications will have few boundaries with regard to accessing the data and the warehouse data is likely to be partitioned on the   basis   of   customer segments.
(4) Market-led organisations are decentralised.
Informating applications are likely to be widely accessed on a client server basis rather than centrally controlled by the information systems department.
(5) Market-led organisations view information as a resource.
Informating applications are likely to be jointly specified by many users who will have a requirement for many different applications to utilise the same data.
(6)Market-led organisations are goal-oriented.
Informating applications are likely be parameter driven with the opportunity provided to explore the data on a heuristic basis.
(7) Market-led organisations have unstructured processes for progressing decisions.
Informating applications are not going to be highly specified and there will be resistance to any attempt to 'freeze' the application specification..
(8) Market-led organisations do not have deeply embedded or enduring business processes for progressing decisions.
Informating applications are likely to be subjected to a higher degree of change and churn than in a control environment..
(9)Market-led organisations are highly responsive to the external environment.
Informating applications which identify changes which should occur in business processes and/or operational computer systems are likely to be acted on quickly and this will create severe pressure on the ability of the operational systems to keep pace with the data warehouse.

Decision making will always be constrained by the nature of command-and-control hierarchic structures because decisions taken at a higher level constrain the options which may be taken at the lower level. If, in addition, the organisation is functionally bounded then the problem is intensified on the horizontal plane. A rigid hierarchical and functional organisation will function in a manner which serves to re-create within the data warehouse all of the artificial organisational boundaries which gave rise to the disintegrated information systems in the first instance. This will manifest itself in most cases in restrictions in access to particular tables of data, in restrictions in access to particular applications and in access privileges associated with status and position within the hierarchy.

It is perfectly valid to employ the data warehouse as a vehicle to accelerate organisational change where a project to bring about such change is being sponsored by the organisation and where the role of the data warehouse in this process is clearly identified. In this regard these is strong evidence in the field of social psychology that a high degree of success is enjoyed by agents of change where the change facilitator first attempts to alter the behaviour of the target group. The target group then internalises the behaviour and commits to the new practice. However, the deployment of sophisticated decision support applications designed to bring about a change in culture is not likely to lead to an automatic withering of the old organisational culture. In the absence of an overall project of organisational change such a stratagem would lead only to turbulence and conflict within the organisation and would divorce the project from the user community.

Chapter 8
Managing a Pan-corporate Project: a Planning and Sponsorship Model

It will be necessary when approaching a pan-corporate project of the scale, technical complexity, and political sensitivity of the corporate data warehouse to spend a considerable amount of time before embarking on the project contemplating how it can most effectively be managed. Unfortunately, very little assistance can be found in the conventional software development methodologies which are employed in the design and construction of conventional transaction systems. In building the data warehouse there will be project activities and architectural considerations which are not comprehended by the conventional software development environment. These will include activities such as data extraction, data propagation, data conditioning and data transformation which will require intense rigour in the manner in which they are approached by the developer. Even at a purely technical level the software designers of the data warehouse will find themselves doing things that are the polar opposite of what they have been traditionally trained to do. For example, in a traditional transaction system the software engineer will, in order to optimise the performance of the *transactions*, make every effort to minimise the number of indices which are built for database tables, while there will be a compelling logic in the data warehouse environment to build indices on all of the tables in order to optimise the performance of the *queries*. Therefore, the project will require a different 'mind-set' at both a technological and at a management level.

   The most logical division of the phases of the project is to divide the deliverables of the system into a number of separate and discrete phases on the basis of the identity of the source data in respect of each phase and to associate this data with applications which can be constructed. Phase 1 might address the extraction of revenue (billing) data, and phase 2 might address cost (general ledger) data etc. Within each phase there will be a number of separate stages, each of which will represent a tangible deliverable. The most significant and visible deliverables within each phase will be the graphical user interface (GUI) information applications.

PHASING THE DATA WAREHOUSE

One of the key management problems to be encountered in the project is the politically sensitive issue of how to separate the project into discrete phases, each of which delivers sufficient functionality to the business to maintain the credibility of the project but none of which is so ambitious as to endanger the stability of the project. Needless to say, any 'big-bang' approach will doom the project to failure since the scale and scope of such an undertaking would be too complex to attempt in a single pass. When considering how to phase the project there are two alternative and competing approaches to be considered. The first approach is *data-driven* and the second approach is *application-driven*.

The Data-Driven Approach

In this approach a pool of data is selected to migrate to the data warehouse platform and the data warehouse database accumulates in size as different pools of source data added to the system. For example, it might be decided that the billing data for a particular service would be captured first. In the next phase the billing data in respect of another service would be added and so on until all of the billing data for all products and services was captured. Subsequent phases would then address the migration of other types of data such as cost data or production data etc. Obviously, this approach is attractive since discrete pools of data, each of which is resident in the operational environment on a single technology platform, are relatively easy to migrate in each phase and the mapping of the data from the source to the target data models is occurring within the same subject areas for each phase.

The downside of this approach is that it may be very synthetic from a business perspective as the decision makers are not likely to construct their queries in a manner that is congruent with the neat boundaries of the individual data subject areas.

The Application-Driven Approach

In this approach the applications which are determined to provide the most immediate business benefits are first identified. These separate applications are likely to require data from a number of different operational systems in order to satisfy the informational queries which are to be executed by the applications. For example, the first application to be identified might be a 'customer segmentation' application for a particular service offered by the enterprise. Some attributes of the segmentation might be the profit generated by the customer or the type of technology required to provide service to that customer. In order to construct the application data will have to be migrated from the billing system for that service, *and* from the cost systems (to identify the profit attribute), *and* from the production systems (to identify the technology attribute). Now, let us say that the next application to be prioritised is a 'promotion tracking' application which is designed to measure the impact of advertising campaigns on the sales of a particular product. In this case there will probably be a need, in addition to the billing (revenue) data in respect of that particular product, to enrich the customer data by adding external data which identified some demographic and econometric data about the customer-base – for example, it will be necessary to know what television region the customer lives in order to measure the impact of advertising on that particular television channel.

Obviously, the application-driven approach is much more appropriate from the point of view of delivering comprehensive business benefit. Each phase will result in the delivery of a discrete business application which will have a tangible business benefit for the enterprise.

The downside of this approach is that the migration of the data becomes extremely complex as data is 'cherry-picked' for each application from a number of multiple sources resident on a number of separate technologies for the express purpose of supporting the needs of a specific application. This makes each application a complex task and, when all of the applications have been built, the chances of having maintained a standard data model of the enterprise will be very remote and the logical view of the data migration process is likely to resemble nightmare at spaghetti junction. It may even occur that different application users accessing the same data extracted from the same systems are getting different results – just like they did before the data warehouse!

CHARTING A COURSE THROUGH THE PHASES

While an exclusively data-driven approach may be described as 'elegant, but useless', the exclusively application-driven approach may be described as 'tactical, but dangerous'. Ultimately, the objective is to support the decision makers in the enterprise with useful applications, which means accessing data *with total confidence in the integrity of the data*. In order to achieve this a compromise between the two alternatives should be considered. The best way of achieving this compromise is to select the applications to be developed on the basis of business benefit *and* architectural fit, while also taking into account the organisation fit of the selected applications.

This can combine elements of both the data-driven and the application-driven approach. For example, a particular pool of data can support a number of separate applications and if the applications are clustered around that particular source data then they should be delivered as separate stages within a phase of the project before moving on to subsequent phases as determined by additional clusters of applications.

To this end, a formula to determine the 'stability' of a particular application is offered here, and in this context 'stability' is taken to mean the ability of the enterprise to construct and utilise the application with confidence in the integrity of the data and the congruence of the application with any other application being developed on the data warehouse. There are three considerations (see Table 8.1). Firstly there is the business benefit of the application. Secondly there is the architectural fit of that application in the context of the group of applications which have been submitted. Finally, there is the ability of the organisation to utilise the application – it may be the case that an application would be of enormous business benefit but that there was no function in the organisation charged with the responsibility or vested with the resources to properly utilise the application. For the purposes of simplicity 3 marks are awarded for 'high', 2 for 'medium' and 1 mark for 'low'.

Table 8.1

Application Name	Business Benefit	Architectural Fit	Organisational Fit	Total Marks
Customer segmentation	High	High	Medium	8
Promotion tracking	Low	High	High	7
Account management	Medium	Medium	High	7
Competitor analysis	High	Low	Low	5
Product management	Medium	Low	Low	4

In the example of Table 8.1 there are five competing applications which have been submitted by the business and are under consideration as data warehouse applications. From a business perspective they have been ranked as 'high benefit', 'medium benefit' and 'low benefit'. If these were to be the only considerations then the 'customer segmentation' application and the 'competitor analysis' application would be constructed first. However, when the other issues of architectural fit and organisational fit are taken on board it is discovered that the 'customer segmentation' application, the 'promotion tracking' application and the 'account management' application share a good deal of source data and that there is also a high level of organisational fit. Therefore, the 'competitor analysis' application is not built in phase one even though it has a higher business benefit than two of the applications which are being built.

Essentially, what this compromise seeks to do is to prioritise the applications which can be delivered from a given pool of the data by taking advantage of the 'opportunity cost' in terms of resources of building the additional applications from that pool of data. In this way the data warehouse proceeds on the basis of extracting data in architectually coherent blocks.

IDENTIFICATION OF ISSUES AND PROBLEMS

The complex nature of the project presents a number of additional problems in relation to the effective sponsorship of the project. A selection of potential difficulties which will require careful consideration and management include the following:

(1) Difficulties in defining the precise boundaries of each phase and ordering the sequence of the phases.
(2) Meeting the challenge of correctly utilising the corporate data warehouse resource and leveraging demonstrable competitive advantage from the applications.
(3) Difficulty in defining the requirements of the applications and in prioritising the applications to be delivered during each phase.
(4) Difficulty in managing the project team's time in an environment which is exploratory, iterative and reactive to new opportunities.
(5) Difficulties in establishing the benefits of running competing queries or designing competing applications.
(6) Difficulty in moving from one phase to the next because of an initial backlog of desirable applications and enhancements during the earlier phases.
(7) Difficulties in maintaining a standard corporate data model throughout all phases and liaison with the evolving enterprise architecture.
(8) Difficulties in determining when to upgrade the machine and on what basis to cost-justify each upgrade.
(9) Difficulties in adapting the organisation to the opportunities presented by the data warehouse and managing the redesign of business processes which will be precipitated.
(10) Difficulties in measuring the benefits of the corporate data warehouse across a wide spectrum of applications.

These problems will require different competencies on the part of the project sponsor, which range from providing visionary corporate leadership to producing detailed functional specifications. This dilemma demonstrates the obvious necessity for *multiple* sponsors to define the functionality required in the different applications and the equally obvious necessity for a *single* sponsor to oversee matters relating to standards, resource allocation, and security. Therefore it will be more appropriate to introduce a number of separate layers of sponsorship. This suggestion in itself presents difficulties in relation to gaps/overlaps in roles, responsibilities and authority which could be potentially disastrous. However, if a clear model with detailed role descriptions is agreed at the outset then this model has a reasonable chance of success.

THREE-TIER SPONSORSHIP MODEL

The three tiers of sponsorship which are proposed for a pan-corporate project of this nature are :

(1)   *Corporate sponsor* with high level responsibility for ensuring that the vision for the data warehouse realised. (There would only be one corporate sponsor for the lifetime of he project.)
This tier of sponsorship is essentially a strategic and co-ordination role.

(2)   *Functional sponsor* with responsibility for defining the deliverables to be provided during each phase. (Each separate phase would have a different functional sponsor.)
This tier of sponsorship represents the most authoritative influence on the ongoing design and deployment of the functionality of the system.

(3)   *Application sponsor* with responsibility for providing a detailed specification for each application that is defined. (Each application will have only one application sponsor but he/she may sponsor more that one application).
This tier of sponsorship will represent the expert knowledge in each application area and inputs from these sponsors will determine the quality of the individual applications.

TWO-TIER PROJECT MANAGEMENT MODEL

The standard information systems development model of two layers of project management can remain unchanged. This model normally comprises a project manager and a full-time project leader.

(1)   *Project Manager*, with responsibility for the strategic direction of the project, the resourcing of the project and the ongoing liaison with the corporate and functional business sponsors.

(2)   *Project Leader,* with responsibility for the management of the project team and the design and construction of the software application to a high level of quality within the timescales agreed in the project plan.

OUTLINE DESCRIPTIONS OF ROLES AND RESPONSIBILITIES

An outline of the likely roles and responsibilities which would be assigned to the different players in the project is provided here and is intended only to provide a guide for organisations embarking on the project.

Corporate Sponsor

Level : Senior executive with corporate responsibility.

Function:Chairman of corporate steering committee comprising functional sponsors and senior information systems managers including the project manager.

Frequency of corporate steering committee meetings: Not less than quarterly.

Responsibilities :

- Appointment of functional sponsors.
- Authorisation of overall project plan including sequence of phases.
- Responsibility for adhering to corporate IT principles and strategies.
- Responsibility for security and contingency.
- Data Owner for all corporate data warehouse data.
- Arbitration in disputes between functional sponsors and the project manager.
- Arbitration in disputes between functional sponsors.
- Preparation and submission of business case for the expansion of the system.
- Capital budget for hardware and software for all development phases.
- Overall assessment of benefits of investment.

Functional Sponsor

Level: Senior manager with functional responsibility for the business activity   in the subject area represented by each phase e.g. marketing manager, sales manager, production manager etc.

Function: Chairman of subject-area corporate data warehouse steering Committee. This committee will comprise nominees of the functional sponsor and representatives of the project team including the project leader.

Frequency of subject-area steering committee meetings: Not less than monthly.

Responsibilities :

- Appointment of application sponsors.
- Appointment of full time-user representative.
- Arbitration in disputes between application sponsors and the project manager.
- Arbitration in disputes between application sponsors.
- Responsibility for signing off all of the products and stages of the phase of activity being sponsored.
- Prioritisation of functionality (especially the sequence of applications) to be provided in that phase.

- Definition of the training needs of the user staff.
- Identification of the business process redesign opportunities and the management of organisational change.
- Identification and authorisation of executive action as a result of data pattern results.
- Definition of the goals and objectives of the corporate data warehouse in the subject area concerned.
- Responsibility for risk management in respect of all activities within the relevant phase.
- Preparation of cost-justification for application effort and incremental capital expenditure and submission of same to corporate sponsor.
- Planning and implementation of system deployment.
- Provision of budget and acquisition of local area network (LAN) based equipment necessary to access the warehouse.
- Sponsorship of enterprise modelling activities in the subject area (jointly with information systems management), where such activity is in progress, in conjunction with the corporate data warehouse project.

Application Sponsor

Level: Middle manager with expert knowledge of the application area.

Function: Preparation of (a) statement of requirements (in association with the permanent, full-time user representative) and (b) functional specification (in association with the systems analyst).

Time Commitment: Temporary, full-time or near full-time secondment for the duration of the tasks outlined above.

Responsibilities :
- Provision of requirements definition.
- Provision of functional specification.
- Ensuring completeness of applications.
- Quality assurance of main deliverable and intermediate products.
- Acceptance testing of completed applications.
- Defining software modifications and enhancements to system.

Project Manager

Responsibilities:

- Strategic direction of project.
- Architectural and strategic fit of system including congruence with corporate models.
- Technical risk analysis.

- Contract negotiations.
- Maintenance budget.
- Communication with corporate and functional sponsors.
- Supervision of project principles.
- Formulation of business recommendations on business process redesigns.
- Supervision of methodological approach.
- Progress reporting to senior management.
- Cost control.

Project Leader

Responsibilities:

- Vendor liaison.
- Project planning, estimating and control.
- Co-ordination of project activities.
- Progress reporting to the project manager/sponsors.
- Quality assurance of all products and deliverables.
- Making recommendations on project strategy.

THE PROJECT TEAM STRUCTURE

The software engineering project team which will be assembled for the data warehouse project will comprise three separate cohorts which will be responsible for addressing, in tandem, three separate aspects of the data warehouse system. These aspects relate to capturing the data, designing the database and building the applications. Despite the fact that the scale and complexity of the project requires some specialisation of labour, the project team should work as a single cohesive unit. The specialisms required will encompass statistical analysis, economics, management science as well as information technology. The project team will need to contain as full a suite of skills as is possible in order to enable them to realise the 'conceptual vision' of the project. Because the project requires corporate vision and perspective it will be important to reflect this in the project team. In this regard it will be worth considering placing an absolute limit on the size of the project team and this author would not recommend exceeding fifteen information technology personnel, regardless of the size of the enterprise. The practical problems of co-ordinating a larger number would expose the project to the risk of developing multiple functional warehouses rather than a single corporate warehouse. The outline functions of the three groups are set out as follows:

The Data Capture Group
This group will be responsible for the extraction and transformation of the data which is populated from the source to the target system. The competencies of this group will be concentrated in a knowledge of the semantic and syntactic meaning of the data on the source systems as well as a thorough understanding of the technology platforms and file structures of the source systems. These project personnel will be liaising with other software engineers who maintain the operational systems which are providing the data. The primary responsibility of this group will be to ensure the integrity of the data which is populated on to the data warehouse. The first and second layer of the six-layer architecture (set out in Chapter 10) will represent the project domain of this group.

The orientation of this group will be largely technocratic with a strong *quality control* environment being sustained by the project leader.

The Database Design Group
This group will be responsible for the conceptual, logical and physical design of the data warehouse database. This task will require close liaison with the separate project concerned with constructing the enterprise model. In the event that the data warehouse project has proceeded without the benefit of an enterprise model, then the first task of this group will be to develop a corporate data model. The real challenge faced by this group will be to map the data on the source systems on to the corporate model which has been developed for the data warehouse and to design the database in a manner which will allow the applications to be built in a flexible manner and which optimises the performance of the database under the barrage of queries which it will encounter. The third layer of the six-layer architecture locates the project domain of this group.

The orientation of this group will be largely architectural and the project will benefit by a strong *creative* environment being sustained here.

The Application Development Group
This group will have the task of constructing applications which access and utilise the transformed and integrated data which has been delivered by the other two groups. It will be likely that this group will not be fully deployed at the very early stages of the project, but it would be a mistake not to assemble the core members of this group at the outset of the project, and it would be beneficial if this core group included some of those engaged in the initial database design. The main interaction which this group will have will be with the user community. The early applications are likely to be simple conversions of ad hoc English queries into SQL and will be written to order for users. In time, as the data communications and middleware infrastructure is put in place for users to directly access the data, the more structured queries can be built into graphical parameter-driven applications. The fourth, fifth and sixth layers of the six-layer architecture locate the domain of this group. However, this group will have to

liaise closely with specialist infrastructure support personnel, especially the data communications specialists in the middleware layer and the end-user computing specialists in the Information Centre (if the enterprise has an Information Centre) in the presentation layer.

There will be a strong information presentation orientation in this group and there should be a well developed *customer oriented* environment.

Data Warehouse Project Principles
It will be necessary to determine at the outset certain project principles which the entire enterprise is committed to, as these will form the basis for focusing the efforts of all concerned with the project and will represent the basis for arbitration on any disputes which may arise during the course of the project.

For every enterprise the goals and objectives for implementing a corporate data warehouse system will be different and these differences will forge different project principles. However, certain issues will arise at almost every site where such a system is implemented and a list of candidate principles which might be used to govern the conduct and direction of such a project are offered here. Some are self-evident (for such is the nature of principles), but the benefit of getting them agreed and written down at the outset is not to be underestimated. The possibility of establishing principles once a project has commenced is remote, since by that stage, a number of separate and different agendas from different (and possibly antagonistic) constituencies will have become firmly established.

(1) The primary purpose of the corporate data warehouse is to deliver competitive advantage to the enterprise.
(2) The corporate data warehouse will be used as a decision support system and will not be utilised as an operational system in order to overcome deficiencies in existing transaction systems. To this end the physical platform representing the enterprise database server will be a read-only database.
(3) The functionality required of the corporate data warehouse by the business users will be user-defined and will be based on the best assessment of business need.
(4) The corporate data warehouse will be designed on the basis of a data model which will fully reflect the corporate data model which will result from the enterprise modelling process.
(5) There will be only one gateway from the operational transaction systems in the enterprise to the decision support applications and that gateway will be the corporate data warehouse.
(6) The project will be managed on a phased basis and the efficient planning of resource, design and integration issues will be facilitated by the corporate sponsor at the beginning of each phase by identifying the

boundaries of the subsequent phase.

(7) The corporate data warehouse is a business-driven initiative with responsibility vested in the business sponsors for the appropriate utilisation of the system.

(8) There will be one data owner of all of the corporate data warehouse data and that person shall be the corporate sponsor.

(9) The responsibility for the delivery of a quality system that will meet user requirements is vested in the information systems department as represented by the project manager.

(10) All issues in respect of restricted access to the corporate data warehouse data for reasons of confidentiality or security will be decided by the corporate steering committee.

MANAGING EXPECTATIONS

The assumption may well be made by the enterprise that a heavy investment in a new high-profile information system will automatically revolutionise the business. It will not. The data warehouse itself is just a pool of data; it will remain inert and useless unless people *interact* with it. Technology is a tool and the old adage, a fool with a tool is still a fool, applies with as much relevance as ever. It is the genius and creativity of people who will revolutionise the enterprise. The main factor which is going to determine the quality of decisions is going to be the skill of those who are going to perform the analysis of the data. It is those who initiate the queries, those who have the intuitive hunch which triggers the first query, those who have the skills to combine and analyse the data, those who have the experience to make judgements about the data and those who have the genius to observe patterns in the data where others cannot.

PROJECT CRITICAL SUCCESS FACTORS

From the point of view of the management and sponsors of the project it will be necessary to establish at the beginning of the project a number of critical success factors which will enable the project sponsors and users to determine whether the system is meeting the requirements as expressed by the critical success factors. The critical success factors are also a useful means of establishing what the requirements of the enterprise for the purposes of dealing with vendors – the CSFs provide a means of evaluating all vendor product offerings against the criteria set out in the critical success factors. In an extreme case scenario, where the enterprise determines the critical success factors to be immutable, and where the hardware and software offered fail to satisfy the CSFs then logical result is to abandon the project. This might well occur where a CSF relating to the cost of the solution was to be stated as critical.

A candidate list of critical success factors for a typical corporate data warehouse project (which are achievable with available technology, just about) is set out here :

(1)   To extract and transfer the required data from the source (transaction) systems without adversely affecting the performance of these transaction systems.

(2)   To enable the required incremental data (from all of the source systems) to be loaded on to the target platform within a predefined window.

(3)   To provide a scalable solution with regard to the volumes of data populated on to the data warehouse and scaleability in terms of the performance which can be offered to users.

(4)   To ensure, through the provision of an appropriate user interface, that there will be an enthusiastic level of acceptance and utilisation of the system by users who do not have information technology skills, with a minimum need to migrate users away from the desktop products which they currently use.

(5)   To ensure that, in the course of transforming the operational data into usable patterns of information, the consistency, timeliness and integrity of the component data can be guaranteed.

(6)   To ensure, in so far as is feasible, that the technological components of the system are based on industry standards.

(7)   To ensure, in so far as is feasible, that the data model on which the system is based is congruent with an agreed enterprise architecture.

BARRIERS TO IMPLEMENTATION

The barriers to implementing a corporate data warehouse fall into two general categories. One category relates to the technical problems which may be encountered, where the risk can be managed reasonably successfully. These technical obstacles to implementation only occur if the project is up and running. The real obstacle to implementing a corporate data warehouse is likely to be related to *getting up and running*. The reason this is so is largely to do with how corporations have traditionally perceived information technology, how organisations are structured, how decision making is structured and the essentially *political* context of a project of this kind. These barriers to implementation, which are termed here as 'cultural', are presented as threats and set out as follows :

Cultural Barriers

(1) Threats posed to senior executives by converting the decision making culture from an 'intuitive' to a more 'specialist' model.

(2) Threats posed to middle managers by de-coupling the decision making process from the organisational hierarchy.

(3) Threats posed to the functional fiefdoms of departmental managers who have traditionally guarded their own data within their own boundaries.

(4) Threats posed by business sponsors of operational applications (and the associated information technology personnel) who have embarked on initiatives designed to deliver querying utilities to their users or who perceive the data warehouse as a reflection on their ability to deliver these facilities.

(5) Threats posed by the data owners of the data on the operational systems who have a proprietary attitude to the source data.

(6) Threats posed by any 'political' agenda which may be perceived, rightly or wrongly, in the mission of the corporate data warehouse sponsor.

(7) Threats posed by the business owners and software engineers of operational systems who perceive the data warehouse as a means of generating a demand for flexibility in their systems which they cannot provide.

(8) Threats posed by the difficulties associated with proving the benefits within the traditional model of cost-benefit analysis.

(9) Threats posed by business users who have already made investments in departmental systems for decision support and who will see the spectre of 're-centralisation' of the information technology function under the guise of the corporate data warehouse.

(10) Threats posed by organisations who have grown suspicion of over-hyped and expensive information technology projects and who may regard the data warehouse as the latest in a series of technology-led experiments with the business.

CONCLUSION

When considering a general strategy for responding to the various sources of threat it will be necessary at the very commencement of the data warehouse project to establish certain clear policies. These policies should incorporate the following key ingredients. A *business champion* who would be the visible champion of the project must reside at a senior level in the business. A *pilot system* which provides the basis of the feasibility of the project. The high-visibility success of a pilot application which delivers considerable business benefit from *cross-functional* data will be necessary. It will also be necessary that the *business benefits* of the project be demonstrated as tangible and measurable and these benefits should be determined by the business on the basis of the applications which are provided and not on the basis of the data warehouse itself, which is only the means of delivering the applications. And finally, it will be necessary to map out the progress of the data warehouse on the basis of an *enterprise framework* which provides an architected solution.

These five ingredients are not going to cost a great deal of money but are going to demand a tremendous amount of effort. When these key deliverables are in place the enterprise may be presented with a data warehouse feasibility plan. It will be a plan which has a champion, which has identified real business benefits from a real application and which is capable of placing the project within a strategic corporate framework. It will be the beginning of the journey and, if the enterprise is still interested, it will commission the next stage – the business plan.

Chapter 9
Justifying a Customer Data Warehouse: The Business Case

While it has traditionally been easy for an enterprise to place a value on the benefits of an information system application (in terms of reduced costs, increased performance or reduced process cycle times), it has been far more difficult to estimate the value of the information itself. The information will, of course, have a specific value as the successful completion of a transaction is dependent on individual items of data being input to and output from the system. But it is in the context of the data as a whole that the difficulty arises in arriving at an agreed value.

INFORMATION AS A PRODUCT

Data transformed into information can have a benefit in terms of reduced costs (through more sophisticated control reports), or increased revenue (through target marketing campaigns); or the information itself may have a value as a marketable commodity. R Glazer [23] has observed the tendency of the information or knowledge component of a product to assume a larger role in differentiating the product. There are many examples of this tendency among utility and retail enterprises which supply not only the service required, but also information about the customers' usage of that service. 'A firm is information intensive', according to Glazer, 'to the degree that its products, services and operations are based on the information collected and processed as part of the exchanges with customers, suppliers and within the firm itself.' Glazer goes on to state that 'truly information intensive organisations see IT as merely the enabler of growth in the production and distribution of information. These firms focus instead on the output of the technology, the information itself, as the carrier of value and the variable to be analysed in any discussion on the benefits in performance resulting from IT investments'. And so, it has come to pass that the by-product of the commercial transaction becomes the driver of future commercial strategy.

Of course, all of this depends on the maturity and sophistication of the enterprise. It is alarming how many companies throw themselves into new initiatives which are at the cutting edge of organisational and technological innovation where they are utterly inappropriate candidates for such initiatives. Just as it would be irresponsible for a gymnasium instructor to permit a novice athlete to straightaway attempt to lift the heaviest weights, the guardians of the enterprise must also have regard to the level of fitness of the organisation.

The data warehouse is a business response to intense competition, saturated markets and the demand of customers for customised services and value-added products. It is the technological response of the information technology community to the urgent demand for the support systems which will allow the enterprise to be genuinely market-led.

However, many enterprises are not genuinely prepared to be market-led. Many more are not under competitive pressure to offer customised products to a micro-segmented market. For many others the issues concerning the enterprise relate to building robust transaction systems and business processes and they have not yet begun to focus on decision support applications. There is a danger that such enterprises will leap into the data warehouse project because it sounds progressive and attractive and will later flounder uncomfortably with the consequences of the project. This may lead to the project being abandoned as a 'fad' or a 'fashion' and (like many total quality management initiatives) it will be harder to revive the concept at a later stage when the enterprise reaches the appropriate stage of maturity.

The data warehouse project is designed for those companies which have good products, mature information systems, sound business processes and a progressive marketing mission. The reason such competent enterprises require a data warehouse is usually because their competitors also enjoy these attributes.

Devising and implementing major information technology projects is fraught with dangers and many corporations have grown wary of 'grand strategies' in information technology. In addition, investing in new technologies before they are adequately tested can be costly and dangerous. On the other hand, companies who wait too long to commit to new concepts can permit the competition to rewrite the rules of their marketplace. By the time they realise that they have been outmanoeuvred, it is often too late to engage in a lengthy development project to match the competitor's weapon.

THE DATA WAREHOUSE MARKETPLACE

The technological components required to construct a functioning data warehouse exist now and, in themselves, are relative mature technologies. In order for the components to be used in a combined fashion to arrive at a workable business solution, it will require a customised approach to be taken by the software engineer. After all, no two businesses will have the same information requirements from data located on the same range of hardware and software platforms. No two businesses will have the same strategies to support or will have precisely the same organisational culture to align with. Therefore, each corporate data warehouse will have unique characteristics which will require a customised approach by the system designer.

What is being offered at present by vendor organisations is 'development frameworks', which is usually a way of selling consultancy hours in the absence of a product. Whether in the long run a shrink-wrapped solution will emerge is debatable, but certainly the frameworks will become more comprehensive during the next few years than what is currently available.

THE TANGIBLE AND THE INTANGIBLE BENEFITS

The emphasis on corporate survival in the 1990s will continue to have regard to the two enduring factors impacting on investment decisions. These are reducing costs and increasing revenues. Information technology has traditionally been good at reducing costs but has not been engaged, by and large, in major initiatives designed to stimulate revenue.

Reducing costs belongs to the tangible world inhabited by the original sponsors of information systems applications – accountants and engineers. And so, information technology systems were deployed primarily to reduce the manning levels required to complete a business process. Cost reduction systems are focused almost exclusively on the internal corporate world.

Increasing revenue is widely regarded as a less tangible goal. For example, how does one separate revenue growth attributable to a decision support system from organic revenue growth which would have occurred anyway? Or how does one discount economic or market-related phenomena which may be perceived to impact revenue streams in an unpredictable, a seasonal, or even random manner?

It can be said with absolute certainty that an information technology investment in a cost reduction project can be demonstrated by reference to tangible and measurable values. Costs which were previously evident will either have remained or vanished. But how can one say, with absolute certainty that revenue associated with a product promotion which was design-aided by a decision support system is superior to a more crude or intuitive promotion campaign? The decision support system designed to increase revenue is directed, almost exclusively at an external, market-focused mission.

INVESTMENT APPRAISAL OPTIONS
Available methods of investment appraisal are not confined to the traditional

methodologies which focus on the internal rate of return. Increasingly enterprises are relating investment decisions more directly to the corporate goals and targets which are agreed by the enterprise. What this may require is an assessment of the impact of an investment in reaching or exceeding a corporate performance target which has been determined by reference to the 'best-in-class' performance of competitors. This kind of analysis provides a more 'real' basis for evaluating an investment in the context of 'competitive advantage' rather than a simple return on investment calculated on the basis of the historical behaviour of the cost and market environment.

There is currently a struggle between user departments and information systems functions over the control of computer systems resources and this power struggle is likely to intensify. For the information systems function and the body corporate there are compelling reasons to use the opportunity of the data warehouse to re-integrate corporate data. For many organisations this project will represent the only near-term opportunity to achieve this goal.

It should be noted that 80:20 solutions have a great deal to recommend them in business, although those cultured in engineering disciplines will find themselves profoundly uncomfortable with the idea. That is to say, when considering the complexity of the overall design of the system, it may be worth postponing the fully architected solution in favour of realising 80% of the ideal result. Therefore, for 20% of the effort and some temporary sacrifice in architectural elegance, the majority of the benefits can be realised.

THE PARTNERING OPTION

The issue of partnering is likely to arise for many small and medium size enterprises where the cost of obtaining the technology and developing the applications is too great to consider a sole venture. The benefits of partnering are threefold :

(1)   There is a shared learning by the participating organisations for both the information technology personnel and for the business users.
(2)   There is the shared cost of the hardware and software platforms.
(3)   There may be the basis of a more strategic alliance if there are synergies in the data being analysed. For example a car hire company and a hotel chain would present obvious possibilities.

There would also be three drawbacks to joining with a partner:

(1)   There would be additional technical complexity introduced because the two enterprises may have different platforms for the source data, different development environments. This would limit the amount of shared learning

which would be possible.

(2) The system would have to be located in one of two data centres, offering a distinct advantage to the partner who could directly attach their operational systems to the warehouse platform.

(3) Arriving at a formal basis for the partnership would take time.

The key issue to be considered in any partnering arrangement will probably relate to the nature of the applications which are required by the enterprise. It should be borne in mind that getting strategic information from data is not time critical to hours or even days and the delays associated with sharing a resource could be contemplated. Obviously, this kind of arrangement would not be ideal where large numbers of users required access.

DOUBLING AS A CONTINGENCY HOT-SITE

Many companies pay a great deal of money in order to provide 'hot-sites' to be used in the case of a disaster. Most of these hot-sites are used only to conduct disaster recovery tests or in the rare event of an actual disaster occurring. In any event, for most organisations, it is a sunk cost. Considering the nature of a data warehouse which is used initially for strategic purposes on a non-constant basis it may be possible for some companies to combine the early data warehouse implementation with the contingency hot-site. This has the benefit of providing an available facility and can serve to reduce the attributable costs of the data warehouse. But it does also have at least two significant drawbacks. Firstly, the choice of the hardware and software for the data warehouse implementation will have to mirror the operational production system. Secondly, the practical benefits of directly attaching the data warehouse platform to the production systems providing the source data would be eliminated.

THE MATURITY OF THE INFORMATION
SYSTEMS ENVIRONMENT

One of the first thing that it will profit an enterprise to do before embarking on a data warehouse project is to assess the maturity of the information systems environment in the organisation. It has for some time been generally accepted that enterprises go through four identifiable stages of information technology maturity. [24]

Stage 1 : Initiation
This involves the enterprise in implementing cost reduction systems which are normally financial and operational. At this stage the organisation is coming to terms with the application of information technology.

Stage 2 : Contagion
This stage involves the organisation in rapidly expanding its base of information systems, often in fragmented and unco-ordinated initiatives. This stage frequently ends in crisis as consultants are brought in to restore some semblance of order.

Stage 3 : Formalisation
This marks the organisations attempts to consolidate and control the information systems environment. During this stage, quality is the theme of the information systems department as standards and controls are introduced and where all ad hoc activities are prohibited. In addition there is normally a new rigour in the scrutiny applied to candidate systems which acts as a brake on development.

Stage 4 : Maturity
This stage is the point where strategic systems with the innovative capacity to provide real competitive advantage are designed and implemented. This is the stage when the organisation is ready for the data warehouse.

A Stage 4 enterprise would usually have satisfied the following three conditions :

(1) All of the operational transaction systems which are necessary to supply the source data are in place and functioning at an acceptable level of quality.
(2) Corporate standards have been introduced into the software engineering function and, ideally, a comprehensive enterprise model is already in place.
(3) An experienced cadre of trained software engineers who are familiar with the portfolio of operational systems are available to participate in the data warehouse project.

Finally, of course, the need for the corporate data warehouse must exist in the user community.

It is of critical importance that the project is timed correctly. Obviously, to commence during Stage 1 would be senseless since not enough data to populate the warehouse would be available. To commence during Stage 2 would add considerable to the chaos and would inevitably lead to failure. To commence during Stage 4 is ideal and reasonably free of risk. However, the real problem arises because very many organisations are still languishing at Stage 3 at this point in the history of information technology.

The Stage 3 organisation is grappling with quality, methodologies and standards in an semi-architected environment. Users are growing impatient at the failure of the systems to provide an integrated picture. There is probably no proper enterprise model. Users are demonstrating signs of declaring independence and going off to purchase departmental computers where they plan to perform their own decision support activities or they have already done so. These departmental systems will create a dysfunctional web of extract processing. Attempts to get the enterprise interested in a data warehouse type system are being ignored because the organisation has had a bad experience of building big systems and no tangible claims can be proven to the satisfaction of the cost-benefit analysis bigots. Everything is on hold.

The danger here is that what is on hold is an architected solution for the corporate data in the form of a data warehouse. What is not on hold is the countless hundreds of little imperceptible initiatives which are, in the absence of a data warehouse, being taken in the user community. These initiatives to develop local mini-warehouses on PCs or on LAN database servers do not in themselves attract a great deal of attention from the body corporate. But the net effect of this situation is threefold.

(1)   Hundreds of users develop hundreds of little warehouses in an unco-ordinated fashion and by using many different kinds of software and hardware platforms and tools it will not be possible at a later stage to migrate them away from their own creations to using an integrated corporate warehouse.

(2)   The web of extract processing will place enormous strains on the information systems department and the final cost in terms of hardware and software deployed or in terms of the IT resource employed will be the same or more than the investment required for the corporate warehouse.

(3)   The lack of an architected approach will lead to a situation where the data being analysed by decision makers will often have no standard meaning and will be of little or no value to the enterprise as a whole.

Therefore, there is a cost associated with delaying the construction of a data warehouse and that cost is related to the confusion that may begin to become evident in the information systems environment. Indeed, it may be the case that a reasonably well-ordered Stage 3 organisation may, under the weight of ad hoc user decision support initiatives, slip back to being a Stage 2 organisation. Or, to put that scenario another way, the corporate information systems may move independently towards maturity while another wave of information technology centred on local (user-controlled) decision support systems will carry the user community through the same four stages of maturity on a separate curve commencing with the experimentation of the initiation stage.

As a result it is difficult to be prescriptive concerning the precise timing of a data warehouse project. Any organisation which insists on waiting for absolute maturity in the information technology environment and which insists on re-architecting all of the data structures before proceeding will probably never build a data warehouse. Therefore it becomes necessary to consider an approach to the project based on *phased deployments*.

What is meant by phased deployments is that certain subject areas are selected on the basis of pressing business priorities and the data pertaining to that subject area is propagated on to the data warehouse platform. Therefore data about customers or a specific group of customers or a specific product would represent a single deployment.

Certain issues arise in terms of phased tactical deployments of the data and these need to be managed carefully in order not to jeopardise the overall goals of the project. These are :

(1)   The phased tactical deployments must consider the eventual integration of the data warehouse and should be based on a coherent subject area model which forms part of the enterprise model.
(2)   The data must not be deployed on a technology platform which cannot accommodate the growth of the eventual data warehouse. The implementation of a phased deployment on a non-scalable hardware or software will lead to the eventual deployment of multiple data warehouse and will lose the central benefit of data integration. Some scope may exist with the evolution of distributed databases but, at present, there is no acceptable technology solution which permits   the user to see a single image of all the corporate data on multiple platforms without incurring a level of technical complexity that threatens the project.
(3)   The possibility exists with phased deployments for functional sponsors to specify separate discrete systems which may be difficult to integrate at a later stage.

The phased deployments should not, in general, be based on chunks of *data* but on the delivery of business *applications*. The project sponsor must always be asking the question : What are the business problems that the data warehouse is attempting to solve? In this regard it is the application which is of importance, since the data warehouse is only the means of building the application. For example, solving some of the problems associated with a mass production enterprise changing to a customised service provider requires that some kind of customer segmentation analysis application be constructed. It is the benefits associated with this application that should be assessed since there is no intrinsic value to be derived from a data warehouse *per se*. This application may or may not be resident on the data warehouse platform. In all probability it will be located physically on the local area network in the business environment. It may reside on a data mart. Therefore, the data warehouse should be regarded as, essentially, an infrastructural investment. The investment is realised through the business applications which require the infrastructure to exist. The applications themselves can be measured against the high-impact business goals of the enterprise, which in turn can be related to tangible business performance objectives. And it is the case that quite modest improvements in decision making can lead to dramatic benefits. For example, an airline turning over a billion pounds per annum would realise revenues of £14 million simply by improving the load factor (on their flights) by a mere one half of one per cent. A telecommunications company might expect to realise additional revenue of £2 millions in every one hundred million pounds of turnover simply by stimulating telephone traffic by 2%. In many retail chains the improvements in revenue that would accrue from reducing stock turnover by a single day is equivalent to a week's trading profit.

REQUIREMENTS MAPPING FOR THE DATA WAREHOUSE

In reaching any decision on investing in a data warehouse it will first be necessary to determine in what key result areas of the business (i.e. what key objectives need to be achieved by the business) would the data warehouse be of benefit. In the example provided in Figure 11, five issues are identified where the data warehouse is seen to have a contribution to make. These issues might have been determined by senior management in the enterprise to be necessary preconditions to improving performance in priority key result areas. The map demonstrates that two of the five issues are located in the upper quadrant of the overall map, indicating the seriousness of these particular issues. More importantly, the shadow line showing the position of these issues three years previously indicates a trend of increasing intensity with regard to the seriousness of the issues. For the purposes of this example, the map would demonstrate no compelling need to invest in a data warehouse in 1990 and a compelling need to consider this investment in 1993.

KEY RESULT AREAS FOR THE DATA WAREHOUSE

Every business enterprise has its own key business concerns which are rooted in the specific environment, specific circumstances and industry specific challenges of that enterprise. However, management science continues to demonstrate that the commonality of the business agenda throughout all spheres of commerce is compelling proof that the *key* result areas of business are enduring and general.

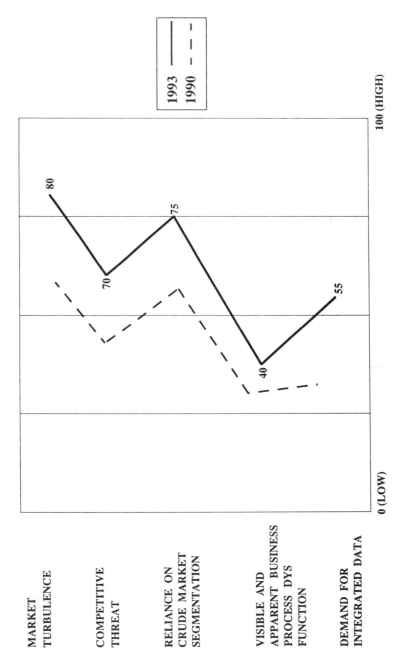

Figure 11: Requirement mapping for the data warehouse

Three key result areas which are likely to be high on the priority list of all enterprises are the identification of prospective customers, the optimisation of corporate assets in meeting customer needs and the ability to adjust the enterprise in response to competitive threats. Taking these three key result areas alone should provide ample opportunity to assess the feasibility of, and justification for, a data warehouse.

Identification of Prospective Customers
The ability of an enterprise to identify prospects and to segment the existing customer base in order to offer customised products is, increasingly, an essential ingredient of corporate survival. To be a market-led enterprise is to know the behavioural patterns of individual customers and to be able to accurately forecast the emerging customer requirements of different customer segments. The objective of the business should be to leverage the data which is owned by the business to improve market share through target marketing and the design of customised products.

The Optimisation of Asset Utilisation
The cost of providing a product or service generally depends on the cost structure of the enterprise. In industries which are labour-intensive, the control of costs will be largely dependent on the production of accurate and timely control information concerning the cost of different activities. In capital-intensive industries the focus of attention is more likely to be on achieving a more efficient utilisation of the capital assets. In, for example, the airline industry this concern would manifest itself in route management programmes. Such programmes would require the airline to identify high-yield customer segments (in order to target frequent flier promotions) and the development of co-operative scheduling with partners (other airlines) or with hotel chains, car rental companies etc. In the case of utility companies the concern about asset utilisation would be reflected in various discounting schemes which would be directed at encouraging customers away from the peak consumption times.

Competitive Positioning and Flexible Response
The capacity of an enterprise to adapt to competitive circumstances in the marketplace is largely dependent on the ability of the enterprise to forecast the threats that arise and on its having the capacity to be able to respond quickly with an appropriate counter-measure. This can only be achieved through the exploitation of information.

These key result areas are not the only motivations for deploying a data warehouse. In recent years, in the USA and in Europe, data warehouses have been deployed in order to satisfy the demands of government agencies for regulatory reporting, but these are special-case implementations. In general it can be claimed that the bulk of implementations are accounted for by the drivers identified in the three key result areas discussed.

Chapter 10
_____Building the Corporate Data Warehouse: an Architectural Model

Before embarking on the design of the data warehouse it is necessary for the enterprise to have a clear understanding of what the key problems and technical obstacles are going to be. One of the best ways of focusing the mind of the project manager is to examine and reflect on some of the most common causes of failure which can be precipitated by actions that occur within the technological scope of the project. Many of the issues and threats that the project will have to circumnavigate are set out for consideration in Chapter 8, 'managing a pan-corporate project', but there are essentially, three underlying dangers with the data warehouse approach to informating the enterprise (see Table 10.1).

Scenario 1 – *the 'Simple' Solution*
Firstly, there is the danger that the data warehouse will simply replicate in the 'new' environment all of the design problems which are to be found in the 'old' operational computing environment. This could occur because there may not be sufficient appreciation that the objective is to 'transform' the data, not simply to transfer the data on to a separate computer dedicated to performing queries against the existing data structures. It will always be tempting, for reasons of expediency, to simply 'relationalise' the old hierarchical and flat file structures and dump the data on to the warehouse. This will solve the resource contention problem, but the data will be as inaccessible and incomprehensible as ever from the users' perspective. This approach will considerably retard the potential benefits of the data warehouse.

Scenario 2 – *the 'Point' Solution*
Secondly, there is the danger that, because of the temptation to tackle urgent priorities, there will emerge a functional data warehouse and perhaps later, multiple data warehouses. This may occur because the data warehouse is being foisted on the information systems department by a functional manager who has an urgent and clear requirement for a pattern analysis application involving large amounts of data. There may be no enterprise model, or more commonly, there is no up-to-date model or culture of compliance. A subject area model to meet the

pressing needs of the relevant business area may be hastily constructed and a 'point' solution delivered. More than likely, the system will decay over time – a throwaway solution without an evolutionary framework.

Scenario 3 – *the 'Perfect' Solution*
Thirdly, there may be a highly rigid software engineering culture and there may be a danger of 'over-engineering' the solution by attempting to cleanse all of the data before extracting it, or by insisting on a rigid adherence to corporate standards and models, or by insisting on designing a full update/propagation suite of software before proceeding, or by insisting on fully specified applications. This approach, which is based on a brittle technical absolutism, is likely to doom the project to frustration and failure.

Table 10.1 The malign scenarios matrix

Description	Environment	Approach	Issue	Verdict
'Simple' Solution	Naive	Data Transfer	Replication	Not Successful
'Point' Solution	Reactive	Subject Area	Isolation	Not Durable
'Perfect' Solution	Brittle	Corporate	Over-engineered	Not Possible

THE SIX-LAYER ARCHITECTURAL MODEL

For the purposes of providing a broad architectural model in order to locate the data warehouse within the overall architectural framework of a standard enterprise, a six-layer model is offered. the six layers, as illustrated in Figure 12, are as follows:

(1) The first layer – operational data.
(2) The second layer – data migration.
(3) The third layer – the data warehouse/database administration.
(4) The fourth layer – middleware.
(5) The fifth layer – decision support applications.
(6) The sixth layer – presentation interface.

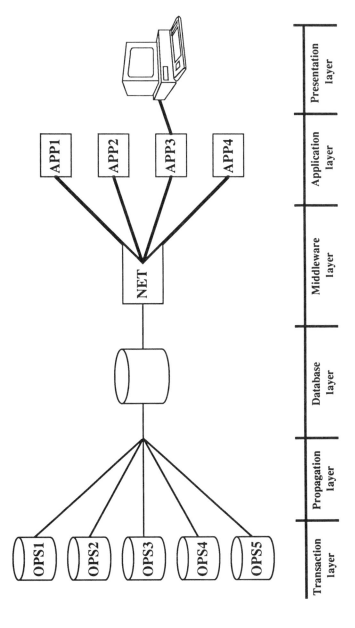

Figure 12 : The six-layer data warehouse architecture

THE FIRST LAYER — OPERATIONAL DATA

Introduction
The operational data layer is the operational computing environment which will provide the source data for the corporate data warehouse. This layer will consist, by-and-large, of the online transaction systems which are deployed in the enterprise. Some of these systems will have a reasonable level of reporting functionality for users and in some other systems the level of flexibility and functionality offered in the way of decision support will be very retarded. This analysis will have been completed during the 'current information systems analysis' report which will have identified the technical and functional characteristics of these systems.

Impact of Data Warehouse on Operational Systems
It will be the objective of the data warehouse implementation to impact minimally on the operation of the systems in the operational data layer. The only software which will be introduced into this environment will be the extraction and/or propagation software required to capture the data needed in the data warehouse.

After the data warehouse has been implemented and is producing valuable strategic and tactical options for the enterprise, then it is highly likely that the business initiatives arising from a consideration of these options will impact considerably on the operational systems. It is the *decisions* which are enabled by the data warehouse which will impact the operational systems rather than the data warehouse itself. For example, if the data warehouse application identifying customer usage patterns identifies benefits accruing from a particular package of discounts, then the operational billing systems will immediately come under pressure to satisfy the functional requirement to support this discounting scheme.

Conditioning the Source Data
Because there will be considerable differences in the quality of the data on different operational systems it will be necessary in some instances to 'condition' the data on the operational systems before it is transported into the data warehouse environment. This may involve writing programs to condition and standardise the data. For example, the customer name field in the operational system may state 'JAMES SMITH' or 'J. SMITH', or 'J. G. SMITH' or 'SMITH, JAMES' or 'J. SMYTH' or any other number of other possible combinations. This problem is exacerbated in the address fields where the town and county may be entered on a single field in some instances and on two separate fields in others. Business names are likely to be an even greater problem because of the use of abbreviations. Linking together all of the accounts of a large customer called 'Mobile Communications Services Limited' is going to prove very difficult if

different key punch operators have keyed in different names like 'MCS Limited' or 'MCSL' or 'Mobile Communications' etc.

It will be important to establish the principle early on that the responsibility for the quality and condition of the data is vested in the operational systems and that the co-operation of the software engineering personnel responsible for the maintenance of these systems is forthcoming.

Validating the Source Data

It may be the case that the data on the operational systems is completely valid and that no question of the validity of the data will arise. However, it must be borne in mind that some data on operational systems must be valid in order for the business processes to have integrity – for example, the bill amount on a billing system must be a valid piece of data. However, other items of data on operational systems are not intrinsic to the operational process and may have fallen into some decay – for example, information relating to the customer profile such as occupation, or customer credit rating, or industry classification codes may not be valid or up-to-date if there is no reason inherent in the business process for keeping this data valid. It is the data pollution that has occurred in these areas that may have to be tackled before proceeding to migrate the data.

This problem will, for many corporations, be quite serious because billing systems have usually resided in the finance function of the enterprise and have, traditionally, been used to capture and maintain customer data which is really proper to the marketing/sales function. Because the data is not critical to the finance function which stores the data it may not be maintained at an acceptable level of validity.

Mapping Data from Source to Target

At the initial stage of the data warehouse it is likely that there will be a considerable gap between the corporate data model adopted by the data warehouse and the many and varied data models on which the individual operational systems are based. An essential task in building the data warehouse environment will concern the accurate mapping of data from the operational environment into the decision support environment. If there is a policy of converging all of the operational data models on the corporate model (a component of the enterprise model), then the mapping of data from the *operational data layer* to the data warehouse *database layer* will become progressively more easy.

Because of the enormous complexity of managing the mapping of the data, consideration should be given to employing a CASE tool which maintains a record of the mappings and allows the system designer to analyse options and impacts of different options to map the data which may be possible. It should also be acknowledged at the outset that the data environment is likely to be dynamic – the operational systems will be subject to enhancements, amendments and redesigns which alter the data structures. The means by which these dynamics will be administratively and technically managed will have be set out clearly for the data administration personnel responsible for managing the gateway between the operational and decision support computing environments.

Conclusion

When the first phase extraction of source data has been identified, this data conditioned and validated, and the mappings between the source and target systems identified, then the tasks associated with the next layer of the corporate data warehouse architecture may be considered.

Because of the dangers associated with over-engineering the data warehouse, identified in the malign scenarios as the 'perfect solution', care should be exercised to take a balanced perspective of the benefits and risks of proceeding with the data extraction without *absolutely* conditioning and validating all of the data.

THE SECOND LAYER – DATA MIGRATION

Introduction

The retrieval, conversion and migration of data from the source to the target computing environments and the transformation of that data in a manner that ensures that the target database holds only accurate, timely, integrated, valid and credible data represents the most complex task on the technical agenda and it is not helped by the fact that it is one of the most underdeveloped aspects of the data warehouse architecture in terms of tools and techniques.

The extraction of the data from the source systems is fraught with difficulties for precisely the reason that these operational systems are inadequate vehicles to support decision making. For example, there may be difficulties finding a batch window to run the extraction suite of programs – these difficulties may be severe if there is a requirement for daily updates of data on the data warehouse. There will also be difficulties maintaining sychronisation between the different operational applications which are feeding the data warehouse since these may be updated and archived at different intervals, making the merger of the data problematic. In addition, there will be the problem of taking the source data with its original naming conventions and injecting the data into the data warehouse data model which will possibly have different naming conventions. And all of this will have to be managed in a dynamic operational application environment.

Because minimising the impact on the performance of the operational transaction systems is an important priority the batching of extract requests should be carefully examined. Running extracts together rather than running them one at a time has considerable advantages if the different extract requests are traversing the same files or databases.

There are three different options for the migration, each of which is different in terms of both the accuracy of the process and the complexity of the process. These options are set out in the following sections.

Data Refresh

Refreshing the data on the operational systems on to the data warehouse is undoubtedly the most simple option facing the data warehouse designer. With this option there is no data transformation. Data which has been identified as valuable is simply refreshed from the operational system directly on to the data warehouse. The data may be changed in terms of the physical layout since it may be resident on hierarchical database structures or in flat files in the operational environment and will probably be loaded into relational tables in the data warehouse environment, but there will be no logical changes made to the data. The advantage with this method of migrating is that it can be done quickly and easily, and in some instances where data is inaccessible in the operational environment, purely because of the structure of the data or because of machine resource contention, then this is all that is necessary. The problem with this method is that it is not possible to build up accurate histories of the data since the refreshes occur at intervals and the old data is discarded. Because it is simply a snapshop of data taken at intervals during the year, it is open to the criticism that events can happen during the intervals which the successive snapshots do not see. In some circumstances this can inhibit the potential of some of the pattern analysis techniques.

Data Update

The updating of data at intervals overcomes the business deficiencies associated with refreshing the data but introduces a whole new technical problem. There are a number of options which may be employed to capture the updates and these methods are likely to fall into one of the following five categories of solution.

1. Utilising Logs

Most database products will utilise transaction logs or journals which may be utilised to identify changes (updates and deletes) which have taken place to the data on the database. Once these changes have been identified, then they can be written to a separate file and used to migrate the changes to the target data warehouse environment. This method works fine if the updates being captured are relatively straightforward, but, can become very cumbersome where the data required for the data warehouse is in a number of separate files or databases and the problem arises in synchronising the logs which are capturing the data. In addition, problems arise because each time the version of the database is upgraded then the programs which access the logs are rendered useless and have to be rewritten.

2. Match and Compare
This is a very simple, if somewhat cumbersome, method of capturing the updates. A program is written to read the data in the source environment and read the data in the target environment and identify what has changed during the interval since the target environment was last updated. This method is expensive, because of the programming effort that is required, because of the machine resource that is required to compare the data, and because of the disk storage that is required simply to store the data sets.

3. Operational Application Re-engineering
This is a very unattractive option for most system designers but it may provide some designers with a fairly simple method of capturing the updates. If the updates that are required can be written to a file by the operational application, then the problem of capturing updates is solved. However, most applications cannot be easily re-engineered and part of the justification for the data warehouse is that it will provide a decision support capability without having to make heavy investments in changing the existing systems. The occasion when it may be a valid option is where a new operational application is being built and where the requirements of the data warehouse are fairly stable. In this case the data warehouse requirements can be built into the application specification.

4. Creating a Super-Log
This option is a recognition of the failure of standard logging to capture the updates in many cases. It involves creating a super-log which separately logs the entire application which can then be selectively read in order to identify the updates which are required for the data warehouse. The main drawback with this option is that it imposes a considerable additional processing overhead which the response time demands of the operational system may not be able to tolerate.

Data Propagation
Data propagation is the most sophisticated option to be employed to migrate the source data to the target platform and is a means of directly propagating the required data from the operational applications to the target environment. Essentially, what is happening with data propagation is that when the operational transaction user updates a record on the operational system then this update is 'propagated' to the data warehouse environment. Data propagation comes in two varieties – synchronous and a synchronous. Synchronous propagation should normally be avoided because it can be inherently dangerous and capable of causing significant corruption to the data warehouse database. Synchronous propagation works on the principle that the change occurring on the operational transaction system is 'synchronously' transported to the data warehouse

environment. With online transactions this might work satisfactorily, but imagine a situation where a batch update program is running in an operational environment and halfway through the program abends or it is discovered that the data is corrupt. Unfortunately, these things do happen and the computer operators in the operational environment will normally fix the bug and re-run the updates. If the synchronous propagation utility has been switched on, then the data on the target system will almost certainly be corrupt or duplicated in a manner that it may not be easy or possible to reverse. Asynchronous propagation is a much safer alternative because the data is propagated to an intermediary stage – this may be a file on the source system which can be discarded if something goes wrong and where the update to the data warehouse only occurs at intervals where the integrity of the data can be assured by the source system administrators. Two problems exist with propagation. The first is that there may be a considerable performance overhead to be absorbed by the source system to support propagation. The second problem is that automatic propagation limits the opportunity to transform the data.

Data Transformation
Of course, it is not enough simply to capture the data needed for the data warehouse from the source operational systems. It will be necessary, in order to optimise the potential of the data warehouse, to transform the operational data entities into new merged or derived entities which are required to transform the data into genuine information.

Data Enrichment
Data enrichment is normally the product of data integration and will occur when an additional attribute can be assigned to a data entity. For example, if external data is being introduced to the data warehouse, the data entity 'Customer' might be enriched by a new attribute, called C1, which was culled from an econometric source database. While econometric, demographic and financial status data will be valuable sources of data enrichment, the increasing focus of data enrichment is psychometric. Because the main source of psychometric profiling will come from the data warehouse applications themselves, these attributes are not likely to be introduced from external sources but rather derived from the data patterns on the database that betray behavioural patterns.

Transport Mechanism
The transport mechanism for the migration of the data from the operational systems to the data warehouse platform will, in most cases, have to support an extremely wide bandwidth and the physical connection will depend largely on the proximity of the systems. If, for example, both the source platform(s) and the target platform are in the same data centre, then the problem may be managed by channel-attaching the data warehouse platform to the operational computer. If the systems are physically remote then the problem of transferring the data is

amplified. It is inconceivable that the data will not be transferred electronically and this will involve an evaluation of all available options. Different vendors will offer different proprietary options which will have different costs, capabilities and constraints. Care should be taken when measuring the speeds of transfer to consider the speed of reading from the disk on the source system, transferring the data to the target system and writing to the disk on the target system as separate discrete steps. Some transfer speeds quoted may simply be addressing a memory-to-memory transfer. These calculations will be important to determine in the context of the available time to perform this task on either the source or the target system.

Data Integrity
The most common method of ensuring that the integrity of the data that is being loaded on to the data warehouse can be checked against the source data is to generate inter-system control totals between the source and target systems. This may require specialised data migration control programs to be written, and this may be a more complex task where the data has been transformed and the semantic meaning changed *en route*. Where the latter has occurred the integrity of the data will have to be determined at 'component' level. This task is simplified by some CASE tool facilities which provide for the generation of file-processing statistics. However, it should be noted that the matching of two control totals is only an affirmation that the data that has been extracted is the data that has been loaded on to the data warehouse. It does not guarantee that the data that has been loaded on to the data warehouse is consistent with the data that was requested from the source system. This level of integrity checking will require a separate control program to check for consistency between an image copy of the source data at the particular point in time that the data was extracted and the data that has been updated in the data warehouse.

Data Re-formatting
The format of data in a heterogeneous operational computing environment is likely to be diverse and the problems associated with re-formatting the data will have to be addressed during the migration. The most common problem encountered in this regard is the differences between the EBCDIC file format found in IBM environments and the ASCII file formats used by most other systems vendors. Depending on the file format of the data on the data warehouse it will be necessary to re-format the 'foreign' formats and, where appropriate, to pack or unpack compressed data fields.

Data Loading
Loading the data on to the target machine can be a formidable task, depending on the volumes and, more importantly, on the service level contract which obtains with the user community. It may be that the time taken to load the data on to the data warehouse database in addition to the time taken to transfer the

data will adversely impact the time available to interrogate the database. One of the issues which will significantly impact the speed at which data can be loaded into the data warehouse relational database will be the number of indices which have been built on the tables on the warehouse database. The more indices that have been built the quicker the queries will run, but a high level of indexation will slow down the data loading process. In some production environments consideration may have to be given to trading off the relative merits of intensive indexation.

THE THIRD LAYER – DATABASE ADMINISTRATION

Introduction
Designing and administering the database layer will be an important control activity in the data warehouse project. It is here that the data architecture which has been developed in the enterprise model will be implemented and where the balance between ensuring compliance with a standard data model of the enterprise and providing quick business benefits from the data will have to be precariously maintained.

Many observers consider the database layer to *be* the data warehouse, but this is a crude interpretation of what is being achieved. The database layer, in itself, is not of any particular use to the enterprise unless the data has been integrated and transformed *before* being populated on to the database and meaningful applications have been designed to access the data *after* the database layer has been delivered. If simply having the corporate data transported to a central database were to constitute a data warehouse, then it would be a pointless endeavour, resulting in an expensive technological display-piece.

Among the many issues which need to be considered at this layer of the architecture, two have a greater priority than the rest. These are the issues of data granularity and metadata.

Metadata
Metadata is the term which is used to describe the definitions of the data that is stored in the data warehouse. Metadata is simply data about data. Without metadata it is not be possible for a user to interact with the data in the data warehouse since they have no means of knowing how aged the data is, how the tables are structured, what the precise definitions of the data are, or where the data originated.

In the conventional transaction processing computer environment the need for data about data is generally satisfied by a data dictionary or a repository. In the data warehouse environment the need for data about data is greater because it is vital that the *user* understands what the data represents, whereas in the transaction processing environment it is generally only necessary for the informations systems personnel to be conversant with the data structures and definitions. It is also particularly important in the data warehouse environment because data from a number of different sources (including external sources) will need to be given clear definitions. Users of the data warehouse will be drawn from across the enterprise and will have been exposed to the many of the existing data definitions which apply to the many functional information systems.

The metastore, which holds the metadata, needs to identify the 'pedigree' of the data in the data warehouse i.e. the quality, origin, age, and integrity of the data. This is an important influence in the 'confidence factor' which will be applied by the users to the data. For example, there is a considerable difference between data which has been carefully derived from internal corporate source data and data which was culled from a magazine article. It is entirely valid to have data from both sources in the data warehouse as long as the user knows the difference.

It is also important for the metastore to hold details of the transformation process, (where data is mapped from the source systems to the data warehouse), so that the users can reverse engineer the derived and summary data into the original components.

The degree to which the data is available to the user in an easy-to-use manner will be a significant influence in the initial success of the data warehouse. There are sound financial reasons for investing a lot of design effort in the metastore. This is because it is much more desirable for the user to browse and explore the metadata (which has no cost to the enterprise) rather than exploring the actual production data.

Data Granularity
One of the most contentious issues which will be encountered in the design of a data warehouse will be how detailed the data being migrated needs to be. This matter should be settled by the identification of the applications which the business has stated as a requirement. If the business requirements are focused on the marketing subject area then it is likely that, with the tendency towards customisation, that the data required will be very detailed, i.e. at a fine level of granularity. See Figure 13.

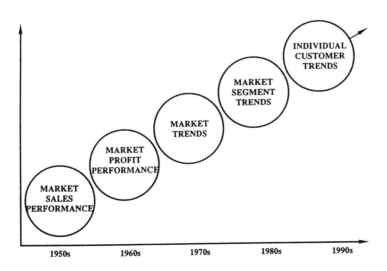

Figure 13 Trends in data requirements

If, on the other hand, the data is required to populate a data warehouse which is supporting strategic planning type applications, then it is reasonable to assume that summary data or aggregate data would probably suffice.

The different levels of granularity which may be defined for the purposes of the data warehouse are illustrated in Figure 14.

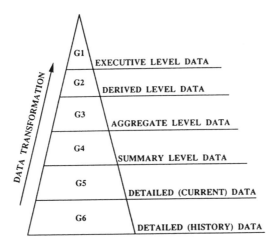

Figure 14 Different levels of granularity in the data warehouse

However, it is simplistic to suggest that the entire data warehouse will be constructed on the basis of either coarse or fine granularity in the data since the levels will be mixed across the many different subject areas of the enterprise. In addition, there will be instances when applications will require the same data for different purposes and this will influence the cost-benefit of selecting one application to build over another. Figure 15 illustrates a case where three applications with differing levels of granularity are specified.

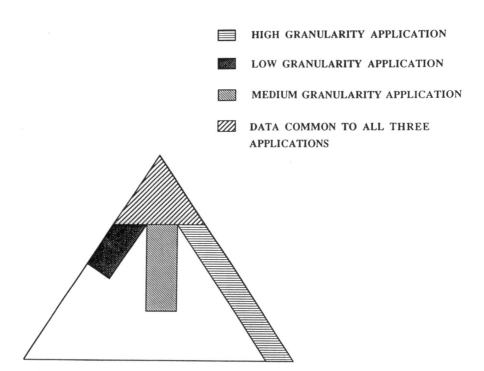

Figure 15 Different levels of data granularity in applications

An examination of this example illustrates how the cost of the application is related to the volumes of data required by the application, i.e. the greater the volumes of data, the higher the hardware configuration required. It may be observed that the extra cost of building an additional application is marginal, where most of the data required by the application is already resident on the data warehouse.

Of course, because the cost of applications will depend on the volumes of data which the data warehouse will be required to support the applications some means must be used to determine relative costs and benefits at the application level in order to prioritise the demands of the business.

An outline method of doing this is illustrated in Figure 16 where a number of different competing applications are assessed in terms of (a) the requirement of the business and (b) the cost, expressed in terms of data granularity. As can be seen from the illustration, some of the applications have a similar requirement for detailed data. Therefore, a single application might fail to present a case for the volumes of detailed data required but the business benefit accruing from a number of applications combined might justify the effort. Or, to put that same logic another way, an application which might require fine granularity in the data but where the business benefit is low (product management) might be built on the basis that the data is required by an application with a high benefit (sales bonus analysis).

THE FOURTH LAYER – MIDDLEWARE

Introduction

The degree to which the data warehouse is accessed by a wide variety of users will largely determine the degree of complexity which will obtain in the middleware layer. If, for example, access is highly restricted or is available only for interrogation by a small number of professional computer staff, then access can be provided easily on terminals located on the existing corporate network which supports the operational application systems.

However, in most cases a wide and diverse population of users will require access via their individual personal computers, workstations, and terminals. It is likely that the individual personal computers will be combined (at least to some extent) into local area networks (LANs) and these LANs may be combined (to some extent) into a corporate wide area network (WAN). The absence of an integrated corporate network of PCs will inhibit any effort on the part of the enterprise to effectively deploy an integrated suite of decision support applications and this aspect of the overall physical architecture may require some preliminary investment in the data warehouse project which should be taken into account at the outset.

PRODUCT REVENUE

APPLICATION	REQUIREMENT	DATABASE GRANULARITY			
		DAILY	MONTHLY	3-MONTHLY	12-MONTHLY
CUSTOMER SEGMENTATION	◑			✓	
SALES ANALYSIS	●	✓			
ADVERTISING IMPACT ANALYSIS	○		✓		
PRODUCT MANAGEMENT	○				✓
SALES BONUS ANALYSIS	●				✓
COMPETITOR ANALYSIS	◑			✓	

● = HIGH   ◑ = MEDIUM   ○ = LOW

Figure 16 Data granularity analysis

The Client-Server Configuration

The development of LAN technology and the cheaper processing power available from the PC have combined to evolve a new concept in computing which is referred to as 'client-server computing'. The basic concept in the client-server environment is that the PS (the 'client') generates a query (a 'request') which is routed to the appropriate database (the 'server') which returns the result to the client. It is explicit in the concept that there is a physical and logical separation of the data from the application. In the case of the data warehouse, the integrated store of corporate data (the data warehouse) will be a single logical (and physical) entity situated in a data centre and the decision support applications will be resident on the PC (or LAN database server) on the users desk. The flexibility which is inherent in this model means that any user from any LAN anywhere in the enterprise can request data stored in any database in the enterprise or can access any business application which is running anywhere in the enterprise. The range of system software which is required to make this access possible is termed 'middleware'.

Middleware Software

It is the middleware that allows an application resident on a client to execute a request for data which is resident on a local database server (on the LAN) or from a remote database server (on the data warehouse) via a gateway. The standard means of communicating between the client and the server is SQL. The client-server model allows for the processing load of the application to be transferred to the PC which permits the server to utilise all of the processing resource at its disposal in reading the data. The development of middleware software is one of the fastest growing markets in information technology but the offerings are still short of a complete solution for most enterprises. The most difficult area to be encountered in the data warehouse will be the *change management* of decision support applications that are resident on client PCs. In a conventional environment, when a version of the application is changed it needs to be changed on the host computer only. In the client-server environment a change in an application will have to be reflected in the hundreds of individual PCs which have a run-time version of the application loaded.

Many observers (and not a few client-server vendors) have represented the client-server as a downsizing option and attempt to justify the investment on the ground that it will cut costs. But the most demonstrable benefits of the client-server model lie in the flexibility which it offers rather than any real cost reduction. The cost reduction argument runs aground on the additional costs which accrue from the need to introduce controls in what is a more complex environment. The additional costs which tend to seep into the client-server configuration occur very often in the user department, particularly in managing and maintaining the LAN/WAN infrastructure.

The flexibility dividend depends, to some extent, on the level of inflexibility which existed at the outset, but it is in the nature of decision support applications that they are subject to a higher degree of change than transaction application systems and the separation of the applications accessing the data on the data warehouse from the data warehouse itself provides obvious benefits in this regard.

THE FIFTH LAYER – DECISION SUPPORT APPLICATIONS (DATA MARTS)

Introduction

Because decision support applications must be built in a manner that permits change to occur quickly and easily, the approach to the development of decision support systems is necessarily iterative, involving a continuous process of change. The concept of continuous change is important because at no time during the lifecycle of the application does the system become stable or the design frozen. The requirements for decision support systems are, in effect, dynamic. In this regard it is useful to distinguish the iterative approach from the prototyping approach. Prototyping is concerned with designing a system shell – a pilot system – which is a small-scale replica of the final system. With the iterative approach the first iteration is not an empty shell or a pilot application or a demonstration prototype, but a fully functioning application which may be deployed in the business. The iterative development approach is sometimes referred to as 'evolutionary prototyping', where the original prototype is not discarded but evolves into the final release of the application.

Decision support applications are fundamentally different from process automation applications and are generally poorly supported by methodologies for the designers of such systems. Automating a business process like order taking or billing is comparatively simple because, no matter how complex the process is, it is capable of being described. Therefore the range of reasonably acceptable design options is finite.

Supporting the cognitive process of decision making, on the other hand, will present the designer with a broader range of options. And, crucially, the process of decision making is not capable of being rigourously described. That is to say, when the outcome of a billing system is 'an accurate bill' then the characteristics of 'an accurate bill' can be described completely, and the software can be judged against this clear criterion. However, when the outcome is 'an optimum decision', this cannot be described and specified with the same precision and the software cannot be judged as clearly.

One of the main challenges to be overcome in designing a decision support application is to carefully balance the need to offer the user the facility to customise the options which they regularly use, while at the same time, avoiding any overt decisional guidance. For example, many data warehouse type applications dealing with sales analysis offer the user on the first screen a geographic map showing the country, state or county with the sales figures displayed. The user may then click on the region about which he or she requires more detailed data. At this stage the user may be offered a number of icons representing services, products, sales, retail outlets, customers etc. By clicking on these icons the system will pop up windows for the user where parameters may be selected and a query constructed. This process may be repeated for another region and the results compared. This may give rise to further queries and may eventually give rise to a decision. This is a classical 'drill-down' application which is typical of a data warehouse type application because it allows the user to enjoy the richness of the available data by drilling down to ever more detailed levels of data. But, in this particular example, the application is structured in such a way, that there is strong decisional guidance. There is an assumption on the part of the designer that the users wish to interrogate the data primarily on the basis of geography. But it may be the case that the most valuable data patterns are to be discovered through an analysis of the profitability of service X among customer segment Y. Now this information may be available to the user but the application does not *guide* the user to this kind of query and to execute the query would probably be very expensive if the data is partitioned on the database on the basis of geographic region.

In many instances the application which is accessing the data in the data warehouse will be constrained by organisational design. Where, for example, there are many different product managers in an organisation, these managers may specify applications which are naturally product-oriented. Care should always be taken by the project sponsor to ensure that existing organisational boundaries do not limit new opportunities which the data warehouse affords to observe data from new perspectives.

The art of designing heuristic decision support applications lies in the tension between an awareness of the complexity of the data and a commitment to providing a clear and coherent route through that complexity. To oversimplify the data and the options open to the user is to fail to optimise the value of the integrated data. To attempt to anticipate every possible request will result in dysfunctional clutter and confusion on the display screen. In this regard, the challenge of presenting multiple opportunities to explore the data without having to navigate through multiple screens has ben assisted hugely by the advent of the graphical interface which allows for many windows to be open simultaneously.

Application Categories

Decision support applications may be divided, in terms of design characteristics, into a number of separate categories by reference to the primary purpose of the application. This occurs because the purpose of the application will usually determine the nature of the system. The following six categories of application capture the range of decision support applications which are commonly deployed.

Presentational Systems
These provide and present information, pure and simple. This category comprises pre-defined reports and statistical analysis viewed as textual data, tables, graphs and charts. These systems are primarily directed at control activities, with a strong emphasis on variance analysis (variance against budgets, targets or benchmarks) and may incorporate 'alerts' which are triggered when certain conditions occur.

Interrogative Systems
This kind of system permits the user to freely construct queries and directly interact with the data. This will include 'query-by-example' type interfaces as well as drill-down applications and the use of SQL for ad hoc queries.

Simulation Systems
Simulated models are constructed for sensitivity analysis and 'What if' scenario exploration. Such systems are commonly employed for forecasting and planning purposes.

Functional Systems
These systems are customised to support a specific corporate function (e.g. investment appraisal in accounting, segmentation analysis in marketing, procurement planning in logistics etc.). These systems will normally be specified at a functional level and will be directed at supporting the management of mature business processes.

Automative Systems
These are systems designed to replace expert human decision makers with a decision support system which can be operated without human assistance or by a non-expert operative. These kinds of systems are used primarily for elementary diagnostics and problem solving.

Some applications will, invariably, incorporate more than one of these kinds of decisions support application. The data warehouse provides the infrastructural basis for building all of these systems, but it is for the interrogative type of application that the data warehouse has proved most popular.

THE SIXTH LAYER – THE PRESENTATION INTERFACE

Adopting a Presentation Standard

The presentation layer of the six-layer architecture is the means by which the decision support application is presented to the user. At the most elementary level it will be necessary to select a software standard for the desktop. This may or may not be an easy matter depending on the range of different presentation standards which are used in the enterprise. Providing access to multiple different types of desktop computer is likely to complicate the application development and middleware layers considerably.

The quality and scope of the dialogue between the user and the data warehouse will be strongly influenced by the style of the interface which is provided. The interface must encourage the user to interact with the data, and the model of interaction must take account of the fact that the user will not always have a defined requirement when using the system.

Command line interface

This is the most basic interface level and would be appropriate for executing very complex queries which would require an SQL program. This level provides the most powerful level of access, but would be totally inappropriate for the vast majority of business users.

Menu-driven interface

This would permit the user to select menu options and could provide a means of allowing the user controlled access to the data, or to applications which access the data. It is not a suitable interface for encouraging interaction with the system.

Query language interface

There are many query languages which present the user with a query-by-example type interface. These are usually software tools which build up SQL statements on a step-by-step basis by taking the user through a structured list of options. Many managers who are familiar with spreadsheet or database products on their personal computers would find this level of interface both powerful and attractive.

Graphical interface

This is the most suitable environment for user-friendly interaction with the system. Graphical interfaces incorporate windows, pull-down menus, icons, buttons and pointing devices. This environment allows the user to explore the data by reference to symbols which are meaningful to the user.

Groupware interface

In many work environments groups of decision makers perform work in a co-operative manner and may use groupware products. It may be appropriate for the data warehouse to populate these groupware products with data required by the user group.

Multimedia interface

Multi-media interfaces are likely to become a common feature of future data warehouse interfaces. Multi-media refers to multi-sensory systems which employ sound, video and animation as well as text.

Hypertext interface

A hypertext interface provides a very useful way of providing help for a data warehouse user and is a very appropriate means of presenting metadata to users. Hypertext uses links between pages which allow the user to join any page to any other page without being constrained by the need for linear progression from beginning to end.

End-user profiles

The presentation options must take account of the profile of the end user and the level of complexity of the queries being executed by the user. For example, a highly skilled user with a requirement for access to large volumes of data across many tables in the database structure might be a candidate for interactive SQL at the command line interface. At the other extreme a user with very little skill in computer systems with a routine requirement for limited information might simply access a graphical interface application which has been built specifically for that user.

Chapter 11
_____Choosing the Right Platform: the Technology Options

When it comes to the subject of evaluating and selecting the available technologies which might be employed to implement the data warehouse there will be a bewildering array of alternatives. No vendor or group of vendors is likely to have a data warehouse hardware and software 'solution' to hand but will construct around the 'Request for Proposals' a selection of integrated software tools on a hardware platform which forms an architectural proposal. This proposal can only be assembled by the vendor when a good deal of information about the source environment for the data has been furnished. This should include, at the very least, an outline of the data types and volumes which are going to be extracted or propagated from the various operational applications as well as a functional description of these applications. There should also be an assessment of the constraints which are likely to obtain in extracting the data from the source systems and loading the data on to the data warehouse. Because a single vendor is unlikely to have all of the different components required for the implementation of a data warehouse it is most likely that a consortium or vendor alliance will bid for the business. The 'Request for Proposals' is likely to be structured in five separate sections associated with building the data warehouse set out in the previous chapter.

The requirements should be expressed in the context of the preparatory work on the project that has been completed by the enterprise. This preparatory work would include at least the following three documents :

(1) An *Enterprise Model* document describing the enterprise and including a corporate data model.
(2) An *Operational Systems Assessment* document describing in technical and functional terms the operational systems of the enterprise and the extent to which they provide support for different decision making processes.
(3) A *Strategic Information Technology Plan* which sets out the strategic information systems framework, standards, principles and architecture for the enterprise and locates the data warehouse in this context.

THE HARDWARE PLATFORM

The hardware platform which is selected will depend largely on the scale of the enterprise and on the nature of the data warehouse under consideration. The nature of the so-called 'von Neumann' bottleneck in the serial processing uni-processor computer, has represented a significant impediment in the development of large databases for decision support applications. This situation has led to the development of parallel processing which represents a potential accelerating agent in data warehouse type implementations.

The mainframe has evolved from single processor systems to dual processors to six-way and eight-way systems. Employing powerful and proprietary processors the mainframe computer has dominated corporate computing for many years and will be the natural choice by many enterprises for a data warehouse implementation. Because of the proven performance of the mainframe in high-volume production environments it is likely to be a popular choice as the data warehouse platform. In most data warehouse implementations on mainframe it is likely that the first performance barrier encountered will be the capacity of the relational database engine. Generally speaking, at volumes of data in excess of 30 gigabytes most relational database products will start to become unstable. In online transaction environments, data is archived as quickly as is reasonably possible and data volumes on the scale of the data warehouse are rarely encountered. Increasingly, the mainframe will be challenged in the data warehouse market by parallel processing technology. Already attracting a good deal of the available research and development investment among hardware vendors, it is being deployed in many enterprises for data-intensive processing technologies. Not all multiple processor machines are parallel processors and different kinds of multiple processor and parallel processor perform quite differently in a data warehouse type environment. The following definitions are designed to provide the reader with a general overview of the differences in these technologies.

(1) *Single instruction, multiple data*
     In the case of this technology each instruction is executed on each of the processors at the same time. This makes the system relatively easy to program but offers little flexibility.

(2) *Multiple instruction, multiple data*
     In this instance different instructions can be executed on different processors at the same time. This system is considerably more complex to program but offers much greater flexibility.

(3) *Symmetric multi-processing*
     This technology employs multiple processors with shared memory (loosely coupled). SMP computers are normally limited to a maximum of 30, or so,

processors – beyond this number it is pointless to go since the additional processing power will create a new bottleneck in the system bus. A query which is executed on this technology will normally go to a specific processor with the next going to the next available processor and so on.

(4) *Massively parallel processing*
This technology employs multiple industry standard processors (up to 1024) which are combined together using a proprietary message passing and processing capability. A query which is executed on this technology may (theoretically) employ all 1024 processors - dealing with the query in many concurrent parallel chunks of work.

In addition to conventional commercial computing which has been confined to mainframes and mini computers (and latterly, to massively parallel computers in specialised data warehouse type situations) there has been in industry an extensive utilisation of high-performance supercomputers for complex mathematical calculations in pure research. These systems are generally scalar-vector processing systems and are most commonly associated with the Cray supercomputer. The petroleum, aerospace and weapons industries, in particular, have used these systems in hugely complex simulation and modelling exercises. This is really a separate domain from the data warehouse as the focus is on *industrial competitiveness* rather than *market competitiveness*. However, there are large-scale similarities in these two environments and, increasingly, similar massively parallel systems are being employed in both environments and this may well lead to a joint approach to simulation modelling by both the industrial and marketing constituencies within enterprises. While the targets are wildly different, the essential disciplines required for econometric modelling in a commercial decision support application and those required for a scientific application such as seismic analysis are not radically dissimilar.

DATA EXTRACTION TOOLS

The selection of data extraction tools and the combination of extraction tools and bespoke software will determine, to a considerable extent, the cost and complexity of the data warehouse project. When selecting a tool, a number of things need to be considered. The following is a selection of the more pressing issues.

(1) *Data capture* – it will be important to establish whether the data extraction tool can capture the data from the source environment on the operational systems where the data is located. If there are a number of different source environments then it will be necessary to attempt to select a single tool that will support as many of these as possible rather than selecting a

range of different extraction tools. A good extraction tool should support all common file structures.

(2) *Functional richness* – it will save a considerable amount of time and effort if the data extraction tool can support match, merge, audit and conversion functions. These functions will be essential in the tasks of integrating the data and having confidence in the integrity of the data that has been converted.

(3) *Standard data dictionary* – it is likely that the data extraction tool will have its own dictionary and this may suffice for the purposes of managing the extraction of specific data sets. However, in complex data extraction environments it would be useful to have an interface between the data dictionary used by the tool and a corporate data dictionary which stores all of the data definitions for the enterprise. This becomes a more serious concern where there is a high degree of change occurring in the source systems which needs to be reflected in the changes to be incorporated in the extraction process.

(4) *Update support* – most data extraction tools are no more than code generators which produce extraction programs which are run at intervals to capture operational data. However, it will become necessary in most data warehouse implementations to quickly move from a data refresh mechanism to populate the data warehouse to a data update situation. This is considerably more complex since it is necessary for the tool to identify what has changed in the source data.

(5) *System software support* – it is always wise to consider what changes have to be made in the system software environment on the source systems because it will often be the case that the version of the database management system, the transaction monitor, the data dictionary or the operating system will have to be upgraded to accommodate the data extraction tool. This will in turn have implications for the operational applications which are resident on the source computing systems.

THE DATABASE PLATFORM

The database platform is a key component of the data warehouse system and, in most cases, will represent a more common constraint on the system than the hardware platform. The database selected for the purpose of a data warehouse will almost certainly be relational and there will be certain features of the database which will be more important than in a transaction environment. Some of the key attributes of a good database product for decision support applications are set out here.

Query optimisation facilities will be important. This involves the ability on the part of the database to re-parse inefficient SQL statements in order to maximise the performance of the system. For example, a user unfamiliar with the data structures of the database might try to add a large table to a small table, which would be inefficient. The optimiser would identify this and reverse the join condition to achieve the same result with a much improved response time for the query.

Database governor facility is a useful feature of a decision support database since it permits the database administrator to place limits on the amount of machine resource being consumed by any single query. This is an important advantage where there is acute resource contention between users and where the solution is to place limits on the queries. Different governors work on different principles, but the most common mechanism is to limit the amount of processor resource being consumed by a single user or single query or alternatively to limit the number of rows which are returned by any query. Care should be taken to examine whether the governor can determine the scale of the query before or after the query is executed. If it can only be established that the query is outside the parameters set *after* the query is executed, then the query will abort after consuming some considerable resource with no benefit accruing to anyone. The alternative to employing a database governor is to build the parameter limits into the application, but this is a time-consuming task that should be avoided where possible.

Concurrency control facilities determine that, where two or more users simultaneously require access to the same data, the database administrator should be able to specify at what levels the locks are applied.

Security and authorisation features are important for a data warehouse implementation because of the need to provide system security, password protection and authorisation constraints for specific users or for specific tables in the database. In this regard, it should be established whether restricted access can be applied by the system administrator to 'views'. A view is a virtual table: a construction which joins two or more tables and which makes the result appear as a separate table.

Data dictionary support will be an important consideration for the data warehouse designer since the mapping of the data from the source environment to the target environment will require to be managed carefully and it will be essential to integrate the dictionary facilities in the source environment with the dictionary on the data warehouse. In addition the data dictionary should describe the metadata – the data about the data – which makes the data warehouse comprehensible. Any assessment of these facilities should establish, in the first instance, if the dictionary is active or passive and, ideally, the data dictionary should evolve into a fully fledged repository containing the objects described in the enterprise model.

Database parameters will identify the limits which apply to the database size, number of databases, number of tables per database, the number of databases which may be connected to a client, row size, number of indices, number of tables referenced in a single query, number of databases referenced in a single query, the ability to extend base data types and define new types, the amount of free space required and the maximum number of servers per system and users per server.

Application support will be important, especially if the focus of the data warehouse is going to be on applications rather than ad hoc SQL queries. It will be necessary to investigate whether there is a full CASE (Computer-Aided Systems Engineering) environment supported by the database, and whether this includes software tools, particularly graphical development tools. In addition the link between the database and the PC client should be investigated with reference to support for 'middleware' standards such as DDE (Dynamic Data Exchange) and OLE (Object Linking and Embedding).

Triggers and stored procedures will, in the long run, be very valuable aids to the data warehouse applications and can be utilised as 'event alerters' which trigger a reaction in response to a given set of circumstances. A database assessment should investigate the number which may be inserted per table, whether the trigger or stored procedure can be nested, whether it can specify an execution order, and if the trigger can be activated, pre-compiled, pre-optimised or recursive.

Load and backup utilities will be critical to the success of the implementation because of the need to load large volumes quickly. Some databases will support multi-load utilities which will considerably shorten this task. Inserting records into tables is another issue which will require investigation as this may be quite slow in certain situations.

Three-schema architecture is the ability to have a conceptual, a logical and a physical view of the data and is an extremely desirable feature of a relational database.

Network support provided by the database should be compatible with the corporate data communications standard and should be capable of being interfaced with the local area network transport protocols in the user community.

Structured query language (SQL) will be the standard data manipulation and query language for the relational database and it should be established whether the ANSI standard SQL can be employed and what the nature is of any proprietary extensions to the standard which are used by the database vendor.

FUTURE DIRECTIONS IN THE DATABASE

It seems certain now that the relational database is the *de facto* standard of commercial computing and is here to stay for some time. However, there will be a number of competing and complementing enhancements and adaptations of the relational database model in the short and medium term. The most prominent of these are presented here.

(1) *Massively parallel relational database management system*
     The race is now on among software vendors, particularly relational
     database vendors, to provide the parallel software needed to exploit the
     massively parallel hardware systems. The ability to execute parallel data
     query is the prize. The field had been left to the proprietary Teradata
     parallel database but there are a number of new vendors in this
     emerging field of computing. Established merchant database vendors
     (Oracle, Sybase, and Informix) as well as DB2 have been re-engineered
     for a parallel world.

(2) *Distributed Relational Database Management System*
     One alternative to the massively parallel route (and the implicit assumption
     that all corporate data is centralised on one system) is the development of
     distributed relational database technology. Development in this field is
     still relatively immature and, while many relational database products
     incorporate distributed features, there is very little systems management
     software available to truly robust and reliable production environment
     standards.

(3) *Object oriented relational database management system*
     Another trend worth watching in the relational database market is the
     development of the object oriented database. The essence of the object-
     oriented approach is that objects (often comprising data and process
     combined) are stored in the database within an object-class hierarchy where
     objects lower down in the hierarchy can 'inherit' the attributes of higher
     objects. It is unclear if this technology will impact significantly on the data
     warehouse evolution, but it is clear that the object oriented model provides
     a more elegant means of manipulating complex objects (video, graphics,
     sound) which may be stored in a data warehouse.

(4) *Specialised query relational database management system*s
     Another approach is the development of specialised query processing
     databases. In one such product (the Relational Query System from
     Redbrick Systems), a specialist indexing technique is used (the Star Join).
     Most of the specialist database products on offer are multi-dimensional
     databases which present the data as a three-dimensional hypercube. These
     databases utilise OLAP (Online Analytical Processing) tools.

BENCHMARK TESTING

In the traditional transaction processing environment, published benchmarks are
unreliable, but at least they are available; in the decision support system
environment the benchmarking of systems is an underdeveloped art and no
comparative tests have been carried out for the purposes of assisting the market.

Because competition over price performance has now become so fierce in the
hardware and software markets the manipulation and distortion of benchmark
tests has become legendary. The following is a list, with a brief accompanying
description, of the industry standard benchmarks which are used in today's
marketplace.

(1) *TPC-A and TPC-B*
     The Transaction Processing Council (TPC) in the USA has, what has been
     for many years, one of the most frequently quoted independent
     benchmarks. The Council includes a full disclosure statement with each
     published benchmark which identifies the cost of ownership of the system
     under test for a five-year period. Unfortunately, for the prospective data
     warehouse customer these tests are not helpful because they are heavily
     transaction oriented. Another test, more relevant to a decision support
     environment, is now in the offing and will simulate a business environment
     with a wider range of transactions and a more complex database structure.

(2) *Dhrystones*
     This is a processor-intensive performance benchmark test used for
     determining MIPS ratings and is arrived at by executing integer
     computations. It does not measure terminal or disk I/O.

(3) *Specmark*
     SPEC (Systems Performance Evaluation Cooperative) is a benchmark
     which incorporates CPU, I/O, and memory components. Two separate
     options are available. The SPEC floating point test is recommended for
     engineering type applications and the SPEC integer suite is used for

CPU-intensive applications. Neither test will fully assess an environment with intensive query activity on a range of data types.

(4) *MIPS*

Most computers these days come with a MIPS rating (millions of instructions per second) which is not unlike the horsepower rating on your motor vehicle. However, it is seriously flawed as a means of comparative analysis since a different number of machine instructions are required in order to execute the same function on different vendors' machines. However, in the case of a comparison of performance between two machines which use the same processor (e.g. Intel processors) then the rating would generally be a valid basis for comparison if everything else was equal, which it rarely is.

A number of independent companies have developed proprietary methods of evaluating performance, but the problem of variability remains. For example, there is no point knowing what the performance of a piece of hardware running a test application is unless you know precisely how it will perform using the database package which you intend to use. Even if the test is using the database product which is going to be used, the database design could radically alter the results of the tests in a manner which could be grossly misleading for the buyer. For example, is the application using indexed files, what are the underlying assumptions concerning the database design, how much cache memory is being employed, is it a client-server or host-based configuration etc. ? The only conclusion that the buyer can come to is that benchmarks are a crude guide-line. The nature of the application is also of importance in establishing the usefulness of a published benchmark. For example, engineering and mathematics oriented applications will employ floating point instructions while a more commercial application will be based on fixed point character manipulation tasks which are more likely to be I/O bound than processor bound. Only if the test environment mirrors precisely the configuration planned for the production environment, then it is not really a reliable guide for the buyer.

The problem of evaluating performance in the data warehouse systems environment is exacerbated by two things. In the first place, the behaviour of a database being bombarded by *queries* is different from the same database being bombarded by *transactions*. In the second place, very little is likely to be known about the precise performance loads until users begin to interact with the system. So that even if the performance requirement and pattern of user behaviour can be predicted the conventional benchmark test are a not valid basis for evaluating competing solutions. For example, many of the tests measure the performance of the central processing unit (CPU) while disk I/O and potential bottlenecks in the system bus will be key considerations in a query oriented system. In any case CPU performance is not reliable in itself since Unix systems tend to use the CPU to handle all processing (including I/O) while other hardware platforms off load some tasks on to other processors.

Ultimately, the only real measure of performance is the custom benchmark which simulates the actual production environment. This kind of test is expensive, but in a situation where the customer is making a large investment and where a shortlist of vendors has been established, then it is not unreasonable to expect that the vendors will bear the cost of running the benchmark. Any vendor who is unwilling to subject the solution which they have submitted to a competitive contest is probably not worth considering anyway. It will be critically important to establish (and publish, at least internally in the corporation) the evaluation criteria for the benchmark test. The importance of this focusing aid will become evident during the benchmark test when it becomes apparent that different options are better at doing different things. At this stage it will be important to refer to the critical success factors for the project and determine what functions are most important to support the objectives of the data warehouse in the enterprise. It is also important to clearly establish what the cost/value issues are, because the benchmark should not be purely a performance contest, with the fastest performing system winning – it should be a *price*-performance contest, with the most cost-effective solution winning.

When designing the benchmark test it will be necessary for the software engineers to sit down with the user representatives and attempt to determine what the likely environment is going to be. To this end, it will be important to establish the 'query mix'. Because the design of the warehouse database is likely to be optimised in favour of the applications which are specified – i.e. the routine predictable queries to the database – one of the key aspects of the simulated environment to be established is the level of ad hoc queries which are likely to occur in the real environment and the level of urgency pertaining to the response times for these queries.

When defining the level of complexity of a query being executed against a relational database, the easiest method to use is to base the complexity on a 'join & volume' formula. This is a measure of the amount of join activity in the query (i.e. how many tables of data have to be joined together to provide the data to answer the query) and the size of the tables. Of course, all of this is relative to the size and complexity of the data warehouse and the degree to which indices have been built to optimise certain types of query. One thing that can almost be guarantied as a sort of 'Murphy's Law' of data warehousing is that a query which a user is convinced is simple, because it can be expressed in a simple question, will invariably be horrendously complex! A rule of thumb which might be used as a technical measure of complexity is offered as follows :

(1) *A simple query* is a query that accesses the (relational) database on key and will generally include queries which are accessing summary and aggregate data.
(2) *A medium query* is a query that requires a join of two or three tables of average size or, alternatively, a query that requires the scanning of very large tables.
(3) *A complex query* is a query that requires a multiple table join of three or more tables, including some of the larger tables in the database.

In a real production environment the frequency at which the query needs to be repeated will be a key concern since this factor will strongly influence the database design. The approach to partitioning the data and building indices will be influenced by the need to provide a quick response to queries which are regularly repeated, regardless of the 'business complexity' of the query.

TWO ALTERNATIVE PRODUCTION ENVIRONMENTS

Where the response times for the complex and unstructured ad hoc queries is not of extreme urgency, then it may well be possible to dedicate the machine resource entirely to the structured query applications during the day and to devote the overnight processing capacity to running the ad hoc queries in what would essentially be the equivalent of a traditional online and overnight batch environment. If it is not possible to establish the precise volumes of different queries, then it would be prudent to simulate two separate application environments for the purposes of the benchmark test. These two separate environments would comprise the following elements :

(1) *A mass access information environment*
This consists of a high volume, simple, client-server query environment. This would simulate an environment where there would be relatively few unstructured ad hoc type queries and where there were many online users of the system who were generating (from front end applications) a high volume of fairly simple and structured queries. This is essentially an enterprise-wide system *architected on the basis of functions* where all managers in the corporation have access to the information required to support their day-to-day decisions. This environment would be simulated on the basis that a large number of information workers require access to the system from personal computers across local area (and possibly wide area) networks. This might be particularly suited to a data warehouse system in a command-and-control style of organisation where many managers at many layers have a requirement for pre-defined reports at prescribed

intervals without a great requirement for exploratory ad hoc type queries. In this environment response times to queries would have to be measured in seconds and minutes. It would be important when benchmarking for this business environment to bear in mind that control queries are likely to be generated on a time-sensitive basis (at end of week, month, fiscal period etc.) and the system will have to be designed and configured to deal with the peak loads at those particular times.

(2)   A strategic computing environment
This consists of high-intensity, complex, host-based query environment. This would simulate an environment where the key emphasis would be on a number of strategically important, unstructured, highly complex queries being generated by relatively few knowledgeworkers. This is essentially an organisation-independent enterprise-wide system *architected on the basis of information* where a few high-level managers in the corporation utilise the system to drive strategy. Only the key strategists will have access to the system and they will have direct access to skilled experts or will themselves be trained in the structure of the data and the software tools used to query the data. In medium and large sized enterprises the data would total tens of gigabytes and it would not be unreasonable to measure response times in terms of hours or even days. The issue of optimising the queries will be critically important in this kind of environment as will the quality of the query statements themselves. Bear in mind that a simple query expressed incorrectly can be re-run minutes later at no great cost or inconvenience but to re-run a query that takes thirty hours to execute is, at best, a grossly expensive mistake. And, at worst, it may have missed the window of opportunity which conferred value on the result of the query.

Of course it is simplistic to suggest that a data warehouse implementation will develop along only one of these two alternatives. The likelihood is that the implemented data warehouse will comprise elements of both environments. The longer-term goal of the data warehouse will be to offer the full population of knowledgeworkers in the enterprise full access to the system for both ad hoc queries and customised applications. But this can only be achieved over many years and the enterprise will be looking for something to show for its investment after a few months. At the very beginning of the project the system designers will have to make some assumptions about the pattern of system usage in order to influence the initial design, configuration and orientation of the system.

In this respect it should be evident to the user community in the enterprise that *some* information systems support for operational decision making is available from the operational transaction systems. While this should steer the project into the strategic arena, the situation will be different in every enterprise and many command-and-control organisations may simply require more accurate and timely command-and-control information.

The disastrous error to make is to offer both computing environments to the enterprise at the outset. It will simply not be possible to devote resources to the thousands of information requirements in the different functions of the business and also to satisfy the key strategic requirements of the enterprise. This is because the task of providing packaged applications to the many decision makers in the organisations will, in most cases, not be a technologically challenging task but will be a logistically daunting one. This approach will also orient the database design of the data warehouse along functionally partitioned lines which will, in many cases, replicate the data problems found in the operational environment. The strategic agenda, on the other hand, is going to be much more focused and more technologically challenging since the demands of the enterprise at a strategic level are, most likely, not going to be automatically satisfied by the corporate data in its current state. To attempt to pursue the strategic and mass access agendas at the same time is likely to lead the database design into a period of 'design thresh' from which the project may never emerge.

Deciding to pursue one of the two alternatives at the outset of the project should not imply the single-minded pursuit only of that endeavour. For example, it will not profit the project politically if the information technology strategic plan has placed an embargo on departmental decision support systems at the same time as the data warehouse is completely ignoring the demands of the operational and functional decision makers. It would be much more politic, in these circumstances, to concentrate the efforts of the project on the strategic agenda but to roll out a single early informating application to demonstrate the potential benefits of the system for the non-strategic users. After a suitable interval another application could be rolled out. When the system has clearly demonstrated its value as a vehicle for strategic positioning and is enjoying the confidence of the top executives, the resources may be moved progressively towards meeting the demands of functional managers for applications customised for their areas. The general tendency which may be expected to occur is that during the early stages of the project there will be some complex queries, some medium queries and some simple applications. Then, as the business grows more knowledgeable and confident in the use of the data warehouse more and more *ad hoc* queries that can be systematised and be automated in applications. This trend, which reflects the transformation of multiple ad hoc queries into structured applications, is illustrated in Figure 17.

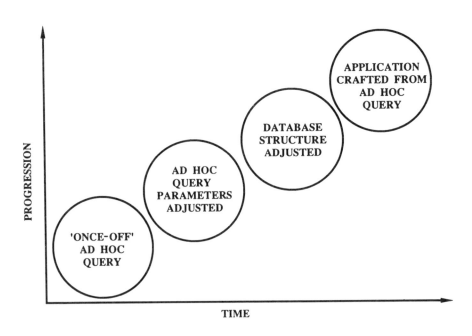

Figure 17   From unstructured query to 'canned' application

It is likely that, as more and more knowledge of the data and its uses are gained by the enterprise, future applications will be designed to alert the decision maker to the existence of a pattern that conforms to a known threat or opportunity condition. In this regard the mature data warehouse will afford opportunities for advanced artificial intelligence techniques in data pattern analysis to be employed. This tendency is likely to result in all of those structured and semi-structured decisions to be captured in prescribed applications. These applications will influence the design of the data in the data warehouse which will be optimised for the performance of these applications. The end-result of this tendency is that all structured and semi-structured decisions which are required at the operational (first line management) and tactical (middle management) levels of the enterprise will be subjected to an increasing level of automation. The eventual query mix will comprise either automated decision support applications or unique and complex strategic queries. The centre will disappear. This tendency (which is in no way axiomatic) is illustrated in Figure 18.

MEASURING THE BENCHMARK TEST

Unless the benchmark test manager can marshal the hundreds of users who may use the system under full production conditions then he/she will have to employ some kind of script-driven simulators. The simulator is a software tool which will contain the scripts being used in the test. The scripts are the queries expressed in the querying language; most probably this will be SQL. The simulation software will replicate the keystrokes of actual users and will mirror the anticipated workload. The test designer will have to provide five components before the test can be organised. Firstly, the data will have to be provided to the centre where the test is being carried out and this data may have to be 'scrambled' to satisfy the terms of the data protection legislation and to protect confidential data. Secondly, the queries which are going to be executed by the simulator will have to be devised and made available. Thirdly, the query mixes which emulate various different business environments will have to be assembled. Fourthly, the intervals between the execution of the queries will have to be set because in a real data warehouse environment where many concurrent users are accessing data the queries will not actually be executed concurrently. This is important, since there is no point testing an environment which is grossly more ambitious than the real environment is likely to be. Finally, the primary keys should be identified for the vendors and a sample selection of typical queries which will be run during the test should also be supplied to enable the vendor to identify the secondary keys which they might build in order to optimise performance. In addition, any decision to partition the data should probably be left to the database vendors. Once all of these preparations have been made, the benchmark test may commence.

Very often, evaluations of vendor solutions are determined by non-technical issues such as the level of technical support that is available or how the project team interacts with the vendor organisation or the level of skill and experience in this kind of application that is being brought to the enterprise by the vendor(s). Apart from these critical considerations the technical benchmark test for a data warehouse system will normally comprise an evaluation of the following elements.

(1) *Measurement of data loading capacity* – this may be measured in megabytes per minute and should satisfactorily establish that the data being mapped from the source systems can be extracted or propagated from those systems within the available batch window.

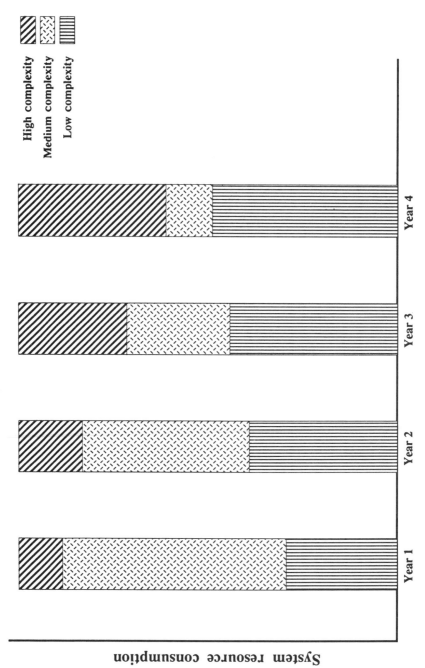

Figure 18   The mix of queries over time in data warehouse implementations.

(2) *Measurement of the time taken to update existing tables* – this
measurement should be carried out separately on base tables which are not
indexed and indexed. It will be extremely important to measure the time
taken for inserts as this will be a key impact on the update timetable.

(3) *Measurement of time taken to build indices on relational tables* – this
measurement will be a useful guide for the amount of time which it would
take to optimise the database for particular queries.

(4) *Measurement of consecutive complex query run* – this is a measure of the
time taken to execute an 'Indian file' run of complex queries - i.e.
consecutive, single, complex queries where the entire machine resource is
dedicated to the individual query.

(5) *Measurement of high volume concurrent simple queries* – this measure is of
the response times on a high volume of staged concurrent simple
queries against the database.

(6) *Measurement of impact of complex queries running in the background* –
this is a measure of the impact on the response times of simple queries
which are being executed with guarantied response times by progressively
introducing complex queries running in the background.

(7) *Measurement of response times from different storage media* – this is an
assessment of alternative response times which may be obtained from
different storage media in the proposed configuration e.g. magnetic media
for aggregate data versus optical media for detailed data.

(8) *Measurement of time taken to recover the data* – this is a surprise test
which may be introduced during the benchmark test by precipitating a head
crash or system shutdown followed by an assessment of whatever utilities
are offered by the vendor in these circumstances.

(9) *Client Server configuration evaluation* – this is an assessment of the data
communications and 'middleware' software support for a client-server
implementation of the data warehouse.

It will be important to maintain the same simulated environment in the different sites where the competing benchmarks are conducted as this is the only basis for comparative analysis and because the vendor organisations deserve this level of integrity to be demonstrated by the prospective customer. This is also an important check on the efficacy of the results returned on the queries – the same query statements, with the same input parameters, executed against the same data should return the same results at the different benchmark sites.

EVALUATING SOFTWARE TOOLS

The key concerns when selecting the hardware platform and database engine are performance and scalability. Assembling the right suite of software tools for the data warehouse architecture provides the key to an elegant and manageable environment. There are a number of different tools which may be required, but the essential tools are going to the data extraction tool (to capture the data), the repository tool (to manage the metadata), the query tool (to access the data) and the repository tool (to build downstream data marts). In addition to these tools there will also be CASE tools and data cleansing tools and project management tools that are desirable and may be needed. The key concern when selecting the tools for staging the data is the issue of integration. Put another way, the key question that the project manager must pose when considering the suitability of software tools is, will they exchange metadata? Bearing this over-riding consideration in mind, the following sets of questions in respect of the main tool categories should provide the reader with a guide to the issues.

Repository and Metadata Tools

- Does the tool have a metadata catalogue where the data can be described?

- Does the catalogue support administration functions, including security?

- Does the catalogue support end-user access for browsing?

- Is the catalogue active or passive (e.g. does it respond to events such as updates)?

- Does the product have a graphical interface environment?

- Is the metamodel extensible by the user? If yes, do subsequent releases preserve these extensions?

- From what data environments can the tools automatically import/export schema definitions?

- What type of user interface does the tool provide for browsing and querying the metadata?

- Can the tool flexibly exchange metadata with other tools?

- Is the vendor organisation a member of the Metadata Interchange Initiative?

Query Tools

- What database products are supported by the tool?

- Does the tool directly access the source database or does it interface to the database via flat file feeds?

- What hardware platform does the tool reside on? Does the platform limit the amount of data that can be examined?

- Does the tool support the insertion of user functions such as the specification of conditional logic or the use of look-up tables?

- Does the tool automatically import schema/file definitions?

- Does the tool supply native or ODBC drivers for connectivity to relational database servers over a standard PC LAN?

- Does the package support business charting?

- Does the tool have a governor feature? At what point does the governor abort the query?

- Does the tool have other resource management features (e.g. limits on number of rows returned)?

- Is there a database abstraction layer i.e. does the user have to specify joins?

- Does the tool have a dictionary that allows the user to assign custom views, aliases, and headings to field and table names?

- Does the tool have a macro language?

- Does the tool have run-time versions? Are the run-time versions royalty free?

- Can the tool restrict access to specified users? At what level is the restriction applied (table, row, field)?

- Does the tool have a local database engine or must it have access to a host server?

- Does the tool support SQL aggregate functions such as Sum, Min, Max, and Average?

- Does the tool have online Help facilities? Does the tool have context-sensitive Help facilities?

- Can a created report be compiled into an executable file for distribution?

- Does the tool support drill-down analysis features?

- Is the vendor organisation a member of the Metadata Interchange Initiative?

Copy Management Tools

- What operating system/desktop platforms does the tool reside on?

- Can the tool import business metadata from CASE tools? What CASE tools can the tool access in read mode? In write mode?

- Does the tool support the emerging CDIF (CASE Data Interchange Format) standard?

- Can the tool dictionary automatically import metadata from repository products?

- What repository products can the tool access in read mode? In write mode?

- Can the tool dictionary export data, table and attribute definitions to database catalogues? If yes, which database products are supported?

- Can the tool dictionary export data, table, and attribute definitions to data access tools? If yes, what data access tools are supported?

- How does the tool import/export schema information?

- What other metadata does the tool maintain and can this be exported?

- What program language does the tool generate?

- Is the code readable and/or customisable?

- Can the program include user exit routines?

- Does the tool support calls to proprietary routines?

- Does the tool create the control language (DCL, JCL, TACL, Unix scripts) for compiling the Cobol source statements, running the Cobol programs and loading the SQL databases?

- Does the tool support user functions?

- Does the tool support conditional logic?

- Does the tool support look-up tables?

- Does the tool support generating programs that perform selective retrieve and changed data capture?

- Can data be merged from multiple sources during the retrieval process?

- Is the vendor organisation a member of the Metadata Interchange Initiative?

Replication/Propagation Tools

- What source data environments (products) are supported by the tool (specify database product versions) ?

- What target data environments (products) are supported by the tool (specify database product versions)?

- Is there any mechanism for supporting the transformation of data values in the replication process?

- Can the tool operate in synchronous and asynchronous mode?

- Does the tool support scheduled transmissions in asynchronous mode?

- Does the tool support complex broadcast requirements such as store and forward for moving subsets of data to successive levels?

- Does the tool support both refresh and update copying?

- Does the tool capture changes by reading the database log or by another method (e.g. triggers)?

- Do applications require to be altered for replication - do they require re-compilation, re-bind or re-link?

- ◆ Is the tool fault tolerant - i.e. does it require that a network be continuously available?

- ◆ Does the tool support bi-directional replication?

- ◆ Is the vendor organisation a member of the Metadata Interchange Initiative?

It has been observed repeatedly throughout this book that the data warehouse project is a systems integration project and requires specialist systems integration expertise. One thing that should not be done in the data warehouse project is to purchase separately the different technology components of the warehouse on the basis of separate criteria. The objective is not to buy the best-of-breed in each separate category. The objective is to buy a suite of products that work together. Ideally, a conscious decision should be taken to only accept proposals from consortiums of vendors who undertake to ensure the interoperability of the different vendor components that are proposed. This measure will help to manage the risk that is inherent in the project.

Chapter 12
The Future: Threats and Opportunities

Preparations for data warehouse deployments are now occurring at a rapid rate in large corporations and will soon become a feature of all enterprises, regardless of size. Because the early developments of decision support applications requiring a data warehouse environment have occurred in large enterprises with enormous volumes of data, a large proportion of the effort which has been expended in the design and construction of the data warehouse has been directed at solving the problem of processing these enormous volumes of data. Therefore, a good deal of effort has been focused (and is reflected in this book) on the problems associated with the scale of the project in large organisations. However, the scale of data which is required by most small and medium-sized enterprises is not likely to test the limits of available technology, even where that technology is not optimised for deploying a decision support type application. Where the smaller enterprise will benefit from the endeavours of the early adopters of the data warehouse will be in the area of more sophisticated data extraction tools, without which the cost of extracting the data using conventional extraction programs could be prohibitively expensive.

It is highly likely (and highly desirable) that, as the data warehouse becomes a mature part of the enterprise information systems architecture, it will blend into an architecture and that users' attention will be directed almost exclusively at the *applications* that are constructed to exploit the data warehouse. From the business users' perspective the data warehouse will become as anonymous as the data communications network. When the business users have overcome their frustration at not being able to access the corporate data they will turn their attention to the new problem of utilising that data.

Along with the technology issues there is likely to be a number of business issues raised by the kind of business environment which the data warehouse is likely to create. A selection of the more pressing issues are presented in this final chapter.

REGULATION

Most countries now have data protection legislation which seeks to protect the individual citizen or consumer from being abused by the state or by commercial concerns which may have large volumes of data concerning the individual. The threat posed by the sophisticated analysis of data patterns may be subject to regulatory and legislative scrutiny and limits may be imposed through these means on the use of data in particular circumstances. This fear is likely to be particularly acute among customers of telephone companies and credit card companies where the individual may seek to protect his or her right to privacy with regard to their behaviour patterns (e.g. what services they use, whom they telephone etc.).

TECHNOLOGY

The current trend to parallelise hardware will probable accelerate the development of software environments which can more effectively exploit the data warehouse opportunity. This may be accompanied by the development of more intelligent database engines which can be installed on conventional hardware platforms and which will be capable of parallelising the query execution in software rather than in hardware, which may prove to be more efficient in the long run.

Eventually technology will develop to a stage where transaction processing systems and decision support systems can coexist on the same hardware and software platforms using a single integrated system software and application software architecture. However, this is likely to be at least a decade away.

Neural networks will feature more prominently in building intelligence into the database on the basis that the constant querying of the database will, in itself, demonstrate patterns which can be used to optimise design and utilisation.

The costs associated with maintaining data in high-availability media such as disk drives is likely to reduce considerably and, coupled with the development of RAID (Random Array of Independent Disks), will make the storing of large amounts of data much cheaper and more reliable than it is at present. A second trend in disk storage technology which will be likely to impact on the economies of constructing a data warehouse is the availability of the optical disk storage option. This form of storage media is often referred as WORM (Write Once, Read Many) storage devices. With optical disks data can be held very cheaply with levels of performance which are not as good as magnetic disks but are a lot better than holding the data on tape or cartridge. It will be possible to distinguish between the core store of aggregated data, which will be required by users frequently and which may be stored on magnetic disk, and the higher volumes of detailed data which could be stored on the optical disks in order to provide an optimum economic and technological solution.

ORGANISATIONAL CULTURE

Most of the early failures of data warehouse implementations which occur are likely to be caused by mismatching the applications to the organisational culture, or by functional boundaries being imposed on the system, which causes the data to be partitioned on an artificial basis. These artificial constraints may be introduced on the pretext of access controls based on security, performance or ownership considerations. Other threats may be occasioned by trauma being caused to control cultures within the organisation or by organisational dysfunction being exposed in the process of implementing and utilising the system. Opportunities may also be presented by organisational change within the enterprise and the need to support a new form of organisational structure.

Because the deployment of the data warehouse may be seen to be going against the trend of distributed processing and downsizing the information technology function in the organisation, there may be a need to clearly distinguish between integrating the data (which is good) and distributing the applications (which is also good).

MARKETING

The rapid cycle of product obsolescence which will result from the constant customisation process may eventually be resisted by consumers in a manner which will slow down or redirect this marketing trend. Customisation may encounter difficulties in a market where consumers are overwhelmed by choice in a manner where the range becomes dysfunctional in the context of provoking stress and aggravation rather than delight among customers.

The competitive wars which these kinds of technology will unleash will be savage and the outcomes will be substantially determined by the power and quality of the information technology being deployed by the protagonists. The intensity of the competitive struggle may lead to a more rapid development of the software components of the data warehouse.

DATA MINING

The use of artificial intelligence techniques to 'mine' the vast volumes of data in data warehouses has become an increasing feature of more mature data warehouse implementations. This level of interest in data mining tools is driven by the tangible business benefits that can be derived from identifying hidden correlations in data that unmask business opportunities directed at offering new services for hitherto unknown segments of the market. Because the term 'artificial intelligence' always tends to arouse technological mystique, it is necessary to identify what it means in the context of data mining and data visualisation tools. At a technological level, data mining may be defined as 'the application of advanced techniques of rule induction to large sets of data with a view to identifying patterns in the data'. At a business level, data mining may be defined as 'scanning large volumes of data to glean useful business information'.

For most of the data mining software in the data warehouse environment, one can real 'neural networks' which is artificial intelligence that learns from experience. Compressed data can be represented as a cloud-like map of points where each point represent a datum in a database or an individual pixel of a video image. Any one point can be analysed with reference to any other point presenting an almost limitless potential for pattern identification. Neural networks are not knowledge-based systems; all that they can achieve is pattern recognition in groups of numbers.

Like a lot of technology innovation, neural networks has its origin in military applications and has been used to assemble sonar and radar images from data fragments. There are many variations of neural network but the most common is the multi-layer perceptron (MLP). The three layers of an MLP are the input layer (where neurons accept data), a hidden layer (which assigns a weight to the input) and the output layer (which outputs a result). The 'learning' aspect of the neural network occurs with the adjustment of the weights until the network is trained to identify the target pattern.
An alternative technique to the neural network involves the use of genetic algorithms which considers a problem in terms of a string of characters, or chromosomes.

As a general rule data mining software tends to be used when it is the business goal of the data warehouse to identify very complex individual trends in atomic level data where the volume of data is so great that the use of standard query tools by individuals would represent an unproductive use of time and system resource. Some enterprises, like holiday and mail order companies, may have one hundred data fields for each customer record. Until the advent of the data warehouse, there was no mainstream application for this type of artificial intelligence because there were no real world problems sufficiently complex to warrant the use of these tools and the pre-warehouse information systems were too fragmented to realise the potential of these tools. In addition, most data mining software assumes that the target database has available clean, integrated, consistent data about all of the dimensions that are being patterned. This might have seemed a reasonably assumption but reflects the fact that most artificial intelligence software originated in academia rather than in the real world. However, now that the target environment exists, the power of artificial intelligence can be unleashed in mainstream application domains, most especially in marketing and sales.

A common example of the type of applications which are being found for data mining tools include databased marketing applications which is focussed on selecting suitable prospects from millions of potential customers for a specific direct marketing or telesales campaign. Because the traditional response rate to mass mailings is rarely more than 2%, even reasonably modest improvements in the quality of targeting can realise massive benefits. Data mining is also employed to study customer behaviour for frequent user analysis by airlines, utilities, telephone companies, and retail shopping companies. The use of neural networks, in particular, has made possible enormously complex analyses to be performed on buying patterns of individual customers and makes possible a level of monitoring of micro-segments of a company customerbase that is simply not possible with conventional software tools.

Because data mining tools can drill across dimensions, (like time, geography, subject, revenue etc.), these dimensions can be included or excluded (or combined) for different passes through the data in a fashion that allows for levels of flexibility that would have required hundreds of thousands of lines of code in an older generation of computer system. The most common way for data mining to be employed is for multi-step passes to be made through a data set in search of a target list. The first step if use a cluster algorithm to find a control set. At each step the original data set reduces in size as potential targets are shed on the basis of successively refined criteria.

For example, a sales objective to promote the sales of an expensive set of golf clubs could initiate a data mining process. This might commence by selecting all customers who have in the past purchased sports equipment. This list might then be refined successively on the basis of hobby, age, sex, disposable income and credit assessment. It might be further refined on the basis of the prospect's propensity to respond to promotions or how recently they had purchased golf clubs. Each pass through the data improves the quality of the list. The final list may be quite small and may justify a telesales campaign. Of course, there is nothing to prevent a user from using an SQL or OLAP tool to iteratively interrogate the data, but for complex attribute qualification with large data volumes the use of rule induction is considerably more efficient.

Of course, when one is dealing with large volumes of data, there is always a problem associated with presenting the data in a manner that makes it easy to understand. This has led to the development of data visualisation tools which are tools designed to present the data that is being mined by the data mining tools. In fact, data mining tools are not fully optimised in the absence of data visualisation software.

DSS applications will transition from being designed in order to allow the user to interact with the data in response to a business event which has occurred in the external environment, to being designed to enable the system to identify patterns which trigger an event in the internal organisation. This will represent the transformation of decision making to the status of an automated process and will mark a historic change in the nature of knowledgework.

COMBINED TRANSACTION-INTENSIVE AND QUERY-INTENSIVE ENTERPRISE WAREHOUSE SERVERS

The pressure to deliver rapid additional functionality in operational applications arising from information generated by pattern analysis on the data warehouse is likely to lead to pressure to use the schema of the warehouse to construct transaction systems. This is most likely to occur by off-loading an element of the schema on to another platform where the operational application can be constructed and will access the data on that platform. When this occurs, this new platform will provide the source data to the warehouse in addition to data which may still be propagated from the original application.

Obviously, the potential for serious design and architectural dysfunction is a risk that will have to be carefully managed in such an environment. While there will be compelling business pressure to follow this route, a strategy based on this approach will be highly unlikely to succeed in the absence of a comprehensive enterprise model and a culture of rigourous compliance with the enterprise model in the corporation.

The most compelling reason why it is not possible to combine transaction processing and query processing on a single database is because of machine resource contention. Put simply, no on-line transaction system which offers guarantied response times to on-line users, can ever allow unrestricted access to the database for complex queries. Some queries would retard response times to an unacceptable level or would cause the system to crash. It is this prospect of the 'runaway query' that haunts the lives of database administrators. For many organisations this computer hardware constraint is sufficient justification for a data warehouse where the data can be interrogated on a separate dedicated machine. This logic implies that if, at some future stage, new forms of computer architecture can solve this problem, then the data warehouse will be an obsolete concept. This is flawed reasoning.

The problem of resource contention is only one of three different reasons why it is not possible to combine transaction processing and query processing on a single system. The other two reasons have to do with data integration and differences in the physical schema that are applied to the two kinds of environment. For example, if the hardware problem was solved, corporate data would still be fragmented across many separate transaction systems and the individual transaction systems would be physically optimised for transactions and the data in any single transaction system would still be too fragmented. Also, the physical schemas would be optimised for transaction processing and would, by definition, be highly inefficient to support intensive and complex querying.

However, there has emerged from the data warehouse revolution a clear and unmistakable demand for the data warehouse to support operational (transaction) processing. The reason for this trend is that the legacy operational systems are, in many instances, incapable of delivering the process innovations to exploit the business opportunities being identified by the data warehouse applications. For example, a business might discover, through data pattern analysis, that there is price elasticity in a particular market segment. The business now needs to offer differentiated pricing to that segment on the assumption that this will lead to growth in business volumes. The existing billing engine used by the business might not be able to deliver this enhancement for anything up to a year. But the business opportunity is now. The data warehouse becomes the obvious candidate to be used to calculate the discounts to be applied to customers in the selected segment.

But, if the data warehouse is to be used for operational processing it ceases to be a data warehouse. Operational processing will always take precedence over decision-support processing. The urgent always drives out the important. And so there is a classic dilemma that must be confronted. The solution is a concept which is referred to by Bill Inmon as the operational data store. This is a copy of the data warehouse that is used for operational processing. It would not contain the large volumes of data that would be found on the data warehouse but it takes advantage of the fact that the data warehouse data is neatly integrated, cleansed and modelled in a manner that allows for the development of operational functionality quickly and flexibly. But the data warehouse remains a physically separate system. This is a pragmatic solution to the problem, but it raises a raft of new issues to be considered. For example, the prospect of an operational data warehouse alters considerably the assumptions underlying the early approaches to the decision-support data warehouse which were guided by the 80:20 rule with regard to design rigour. If the decision-support data warehouse is ever to be used as the basis of operational processing a great deal more emphasis needs to be laid on the data quality, data modelling and data integrity issues.

Very fundamental issues of information technology architecture are also raised by the operational data warehouse since it challenges traditional assumptions, based on CASE and repository technologies, concerning the integration of operational systems. There are implications here too for the CASE vendors who may re-align their products to focus on the data mapping activities that are necessary to realise the data warehouse vision, rather than pursuing the stalled initiative of enterprise-wide application integration via the traditional repository route.

The economic case for an operational transaction-oriented data warehouse is clear. Reducing the 'time-to-market' for new products and services represents the main argument for such a system. The operational data warehouse also raises an intriguing prospect of the 'disposable application'. Many operational applications in the sales/marketing/strategic planning domains would have a limited life-span because they would be associated with a specific sales promotion, marketing campaign or planning cycle. The likelihood is that the operational data warehouse would have rule-based data which would provide a flexible kernel for all of the operational applications. The application might have re-usable components but, in many instances, would not be a permanent application supporting a permanent activity.

What is clear about the operational data warehouse is that it is an inevitable consequence of having a decision-support data warehouse. It can also be asserted confidently that an operational data warehouse and a decision support data warehouse will, for the foreseeable future, be resident on separate computers and will probably have physical schemas that will diverge considerable over time. It can also be anticipated that a considerable amount of new operational functionality will be added, in future, via the operational data warehouse.

If the decision-support data warehouse does spawn the operational data warehouse, then the operational data warehouse cannot expect to continue to exist indefinitely as an a platform for the development of ad hoc operational applications. It will eventually evolve into a platform that will provide all of the functionality within the subject-area of the operational data warehouse as the older legacy operational systems are shed by their enterprise. What will then emerge will be subject-oriented enterprise servers which will support all of the operational requirements of each of the subject-areas of the enterprise.

Somewhere in the course of this evolution the operational data warehouse will cease to be a product of the decision-support data warehouse and will, instead, become the main source of data feeding the decision-support data warehouse. What may eventually emerge from this evolution is a single operational enterprise server for the entire corporation or even a single combined operational/decision-support enterprise server that will realise the ideal vision of the 'single corporate database'. But this vision is, at least, a decade away.

Ultimately the vision of an operational data warehouse or an enterprise server is not enabled or constrained by technological issues but it is, in fact, a design and architectural issue. The main impediments to creating an operational data warehouse out of a decision-support data warehouse relate to methodology, project management and architectural clarity for this new environment.

CLIENT-SERVER

While data warehousing presents an ideal opportunity for an enterprise to implement a large client-server system without the complications of an operational environment, the constraints of client server computing do eventually have to be confronted. It is true that most vendor organisations are now producing more robust, reliable client-server versions of their technologies but there is still ample potential to become entangled in an expensive failed project because of the relative immaturity of the client-server model of computing. For example, client server computing has proven much more expensive than was first envisaged and the cost of ownership of a complex architecture comprising multiple tools at multiple locations cannot be underestimated.

Another common problem associated with client-server computing generally, and with data warehousing in particular, relates to the difficulties encountered in managing a multi-vendor project. This potential headache is best addressed by inviting proposals for a data warehousing solution from multiple vendors and by indicating that a preference exists for a lead vendor to present an integrated proposal from multiple suppliers. In addition, it is reasonable to include penalty clauses in respect of non-compliance with the specification supplied to the consortium. This means that the headaches, if there are any, will have to be tackled by the lead contractor who is likely to ensure, before submitting a proposal, that all of the technical components and organisational units of the different parties work effectively together.

But perhaps the most worrying aspect of client-server computing relates to security, or the absence of security. At present, the only practical options exist in the middleware layer through the use of database utilities or remote procedure calls. The middleware intercepts requests sent by the client to the server in order to ascertain the legitimacy of the request and, if the request is found to be legitimate, the query is allowed to proceed. This is a patently inadequate long-term strategy for security on mission critical systems.

VENDOR STABILITY

Like all new marketplaces, data warehousing has spawned new vendors providing niche solutions to the data warehouse problem as well as a plethora of new products and services from established vendors. There are, for example, at the time of going to print over sixty different query tool vendors of SQL, OLAP and other specialised tools. It is clear that this situation, while it is desirable in the short term, cannot continue indefinitely. Considerable consolidation can be expected in this marketplace. This is likely to occur by degrees with formal partnerships being formed in the early stages which will mature into takeovers and mergers over time. The end result is likely to simplify the data warehouse architecture as both the data extraction and middleware layers are, to some extent, synthetic. The entire copy management/data extraction activity is really proper to the database utility suite and will eventually reside there. Middleware is really a feature that should belong to the operating system and/or the query tool that is interrogating the database. Middleware, as we know it today, will eventually become embedded in the operating system and disappear as a separate activity.

The Object Management Group has now defined the COBRA (Common Object Request Broker Architecture) standard for inter-working applications to operate across multiple platforms. And, increasingly, the presentation layer will become irrelevant. Internet-driven developments such as Sun's Java computer language, creates a 'virtual' machine which allows any computer to simulate a Java environment. These developments, along with other Internet innovations like the 'disposable application' will make it possible for users to generate programmes from any kind of query environment on any kind of desktop hardware to access the data warehouse server.

One of the main effects of the data warehouse revolution in the information technology marketplace has been the rejuvenation of near-dormant product lines.

For example, the multi-dimensional database is not new. But the growth of such business analysis engines was retarded by the inability of the enterprise to populate good quality data on to such database products. Another sphere of computing that has been re-awakened is artificial intelligence, which had been languishing as a solution in search of a problem. Now that there are warehouses crammed with data the need for intelligent pattern analysis tools has become apparent. Front-end tool vendors are also enjoying real growth. There was always a limit imposed on the number of query tool licences by the fact that only a very limited number of users could be allowed access to the operational databases. Now this constraint no longer exists. The concept of the Information Centre had gone as far as it could go in enabling end-user computing, but now the data warehouse will take over where the Information Centre left off. But perhaps the real winners have been the hardware platform vendors and relational database vendors who have enjoyed a real windfall from the additional systems requirements brought about by data replication.

As progress is made in the rationalisation of product offerings the likelihood is that a more 'shrink-wrapped' data warehouse will become available from a small number (three or four?) of leading suppliers who will have managed to assemble an integrated set of products. The implications of this development is that organisations that are now building data warehouses must be reconciled with the fact that it will be necessary for them to discard tools that they select now as these tool vendors fade from the marketplace or are consolidated with other products that are incompatible with wider corporate standards.

The only part of the data warehouse that should be considered critical in the medium-term is the database product. Certainly the query tools should be considered to be tactical acquisitions which are likely to be discarded at a later stage. Achieving a good fit in the medium-term between the data management products and the copy management products can be considered as a considerable achievement. And, in this marketplace, at this time, there is no long-term.

METADATA STANDARDS

Metadata is the 'glue' that binds the data warehouse together. To the extent that data warehousing is a new and distinct category of software engineering, it is the need for metadata management that bestows that novelty. Every other aspect of data warehousing has been happening in some shape or form for some considerable time. There are no skills shortages in the marketplace in the art of data modelling, database design, data staging, extract processing, query tools or GUI application development. Assembling all of these skills in a complex systems integration project is very challenging and requiring of special project management techniques, but it would not require fundamentally new skills. But metadata management is a new concept because data warehousing is leading to a degree of data transformation and migration that is unprecedented. Some means must be created to manage the movement of the data from operational legacy systems and external data sources to the data warehouse and onwards to the data marts and DSS applications.

If one is ever in doubt that something genuinely new is happening one should look to the organisational structure of the IS department and observe if anything has really changed. And what has emerged from data warehousing is a new kind of job description: the Data Steward. The Data Steward is a new kind of software professional that has a much wider brief than the conventional database administrator or data architect. An organisation tended to have many database administrators for the many different systems in the enterprise and the data architect (where one existed) tended to be confined to the domain of modelling and strategy rather than systems development or operation. The Data Steward is at the centre of the operation of the decision support systems because the data steward is concerned with managing the metadata across the entire enterprise. This is fundamentally new and, because of that, there are no adequate tools to help the Data Steward to administer the overall data warehouse architecture.

At this stage in the evolution of data warehousing metadata management is the weak link in the system and everyone involved in data warehousing knows this to be true. The only means of replicating the data about the data in the current environment are cumbersome and unwieldy. The data from the source systems data dictionary (which are likely to be Cobol copybooks) must be manually populated on to the dictionary associated with the copy management tool and the data that is loaded on to the data warehouse must be described to the relational database catalogue and again the metadata must be entered on the front-end tool repository. The process of data staging cannot be automated until each of these four components interact. None of the tool vendors in this market offers a truly useful information catalogue for end-users to use as a means of comprehending the data.

The industry has responded to this problem by forming, in October 1995, the Metadata Interchange Initiative which is administered by the Metadata Council. The charter of the Metadata Council is "to develop the standard specifications for metadata interchange format and its support mechanism". The Metadata Council has clearly stated that it is not a standards specification body but sees its goal as defining an extensible mechanism that allows different vendors to exchange common metadata. In essence, what this means is that the Council will create a vendor-independent, industry-defined and maintained standard *access* mechanism and standard application programming interface (API) for metadata. All those vendors whose products create, access or are dependent on metadata participate on the Council and the initial specification that is agreed by the Council represents the common denominator that all Council member vendors agree to support.

The interchange standard also provides for an approved set of optional extension components that are relevant only to a particular type or class of tool or a specific application or architecture. The Metadata Interchange Standard draws a distinction between the *Application Metamodel* which contains the tables etc. used to "hold" the metadata for schemas etc. for a particular application and the *Metadata Metamodel* which is the set of objects that the Metadata Interchange

Standard can be used to describe. These metamodels will assist considerably in achieving the goal of metadata replication across all of the tools that need to know the metadata of a data warehouse. This is the internal view of the metadata that the data steward needs to manage the environment.

But there is also an external view of metadata that the end-user needs to have access to in order to understand the data in the data warehouse. This view of the metadata is commonly referred to as the Information Catalogue which is the business information directory of the data warehouse. The Information Catalogue is the essential link between the data warehouse users (and their tools) and the data in the warehouse and it may simply be a passive directory that users can browse or it can be an active Catalogue that supports more advanced functions.

The Catalogue might include administration functions which manage security and access functions and may be used to log usage and performance metrics. But the main purpose of the Catalogue is to provide data about the data in the warehouse so that the user feels empowered to exploit that data. The Catalogue should have both a logical and a physical view of the data so that the user can browse at database, table and column level as well as at subject-area, entity and attribute level. Business definitions of the data as well as any business rules associate with the data will need to be captured in the Catalogue.

As well as a browser function the Catalogue should have a search function to allow the user to define a search string and a request function that allows the user to build an SQL request to select data to be moved from the data warehouse to a local server or data mart. A very sophisticated Catalogue might support the scheduled movement of data sub-sets from the data warehouse to local applications and data marts and might also provide event monitors which notify the Catalogue upon the completion of extraction and replication tasks. In a mature data warehouse environment where there are complex layers of extract processing and complex webs of data marts (and possibly interweaved operational processing) the need for an active metadata Information Catalogue becomes acute. Such an active catalogue becomes the nerve centre of the data warehouse and will need to have application programming interfaces to the CASE, repository, extraction and query tools.

The Catalogue should provide the user with a full map of the data warehouse environment with built-in help functions. Most enterprises have had to build their own Catalogues and will have a vested interest in the success of the Metadata Interchange Initiative because it concerns the corporate developers of Information Catalogues every bit as much as the vendor community.

The Metadata Interchange Initiative is supported by most of the leading vendors of data discovery tools, copy management tools, CASE tools, replication tools, user query tools and database servers. The best hope for data warehousing is that the Council quickly evolves interchange standards that achieve widespread compliance. When this happens the data warehouse market, and the degree of integration of the products in that market, will mature rapidly.

FUTURE DATABASE TECHNOLOGY

The relational database model is, at present, the only enterprise-strength product available as the engine of the data warehouse, particularly for the management of large volumes of data. However, it is widely acknowledged that it is not the ideal model for a query-intensive environment. Ted Codd, who was the originator of the relational model is clear on this point. In 1995 he wrote that "relational DBMS were never intended to provide the very powerful functions for data synthesis, analysis, and consolidation that is being defined as multi-dimensional analysis." He goes on to say that "these types of functions were always intended to be provided by separate, end-user tools that were outside and complementary to the relational DBMS products." Codd then goes on to define 12 rules for on-line analytical processing (OLAP) which are highlighted hereunder :

1. Multidimensional conceptual view
2. Transparency
3. Accessibility
4. Consistent reporting performance
5. Client-server architecture
6. Generic dimensionality
7. Dynamic sparse matrix handling
8. Multi-user support
9. Unrestricted cross-dimensional calculations
10. Intuitive data manipulation
11. Flexible reporting
12. Unlimited dimensions/aggregation levels

Codd's observations on the constraints of the relational database are, more properly, a reflection of the constrains of SQL, which was not originated by Codd. Most business queries are, by their nature, multi-dimensional and the more common dimensions are product, market, location and time (e.g. 'how many widgets were sold to the retail sector in France in September'?). Business queries also require, typically, some level of ordering and averaging of the data, and SQL is an awkward tool in the service of this kind of business analysis.

SQL's weaknesses include poor support for statistical analysis (e.g. calculating a variance or a standard deviation), a failure to support running averages (e.g. ordering the top 10 customers), and supporting sequenced data (e.g. data for the last six months). Standard SQL is a set-oriented language and all operations are defined to operate on un-ordered, or indeterminately ordered, data. Because SQL can only perform sorting after all other processing is completed, any sophisticated analysis has to be done on the client. This two-stage process is inefficient and places a great strain on the network capabilities because of the need to move large volumes of raw data from the server (where it has been selected using SQL), to the client, (where it will be analysed using a separate query tool).

Of course, SQL bigots will argue that these kinds of queries can be supported by SQL (with the same vehemence that PL1 bigots will muster to support their contention that there is no need for copy management tools), which all goes to demonstrate that Heath Robinson is alive and well. But those tasked with accountability for the cost of ownership of the data warehouse must beware of the homemade solution where there is a viable alternative. SQL can be used to get the data that is required from the database and processing algorithms can be used at the client end to provide the answers to complex business queries but an OLAP data mart may be a much more elegant solution. Because OLAP relies on models, or outlines, defined by multiple dimensions rather than by a series of joined tables, it presents a more recognisable picture to the business user.

Dimensions are composed of members which are units of a dimension. For example, 'month' may be a member of the dimension 'time'. Because the OLAP databases will pre-analyse the potential intersections between elements in the model, it can provide pre-packed consolidations and aggregations. When an OLAP user generates a query against an OLAP database the database finds the intersection of dimension members within a matrix and retrieves only that data set. This is considerably more efficient than the relational database where an I/O intensive sequential read of the tables to be joined would have to occur.

Of course, there is a down-side to using OLAP databases. One constraint has to do with the volume of data that can be handled; there is general agreement that data volumes over 10 gigabytes are not recommended. In addition, the OLAP databases have weak development environments and usually presents the user with a spreadsheet-style interface. Also, it must be recognised that certain kinds of query are not multi-dimensional and some ad hoc complex queries are still better supported by SQL. But the main value of SQL lies in its standardisation which permits interoperability with a wide range of other products. Therefore, it is likely that SQL and OLAP will co-exist for the foreseeable future.

Some new developments can be expected in the relational database model, as well as in SQL, to meet the needs of data warehousing. The main thrust of relational database vendor research in the past decade has been directed at improving transaction performance throughput. The target has long been the TPC benchmark tests. But, as databases became more and more efficient at getting the data into the databases, more and more design decisions were made that compromised the ability of the user to get data out of the database.

Now that data warehousing is entering mainstream computing, enhancements to the relational model to accommodate this market can be expected. These will include more sophisticated resource management utilities to manage 'runaway' queries as well as performance tuning utilities for the intensive querying environment which allows queries to be optimised by reference to physical schemas, access paths, disk layouts and indices. There will also need to be seamless dimensional integration between relational database products and multidimensional database products which reflects the reality of current corporate architectures. This will require relational database data to be consistent with the multidimensional data so that the detailed tables of data on the enterprise server can be 'rolled up' into the summary/aggregate data contained on the multidimensional database.

The new SQL standard which will be unveiled in 1997 may take account of some of the deficiencies in the current standard and may provide support for multi-media and for user-defined data types (both of which are sorely needed in the data warehouse environment). But there is a large question mark over the backward compatibility of such a new standard with existing SQL.

CONCLUSION

Access to data has been, historically, a technical problem for the software engineers and a psychological problem for the business users of software systems. Over the past decades many of the proud achievements of the information systems designers have left information systems users cold. For many business users, the fact that access to the data was only a one-week training course away was sufficiently daunting that it might as well have been a universe away. The general workforce were trained to use dumb terminals to perform highly systematic tasks on applications where there was a very limited ability to get lost. Truly useful decision support systems could not be structured quite like that. Decision support systems had to offer an almost infinite flexibility to the user and it was the complexity inherent in that flexibility that created the problem. It was a measure of just how desperate the computer industry was that SQL got labelled a 'user tool'. SQL is not a user tool – not for the average user anyway. Grappling with computer languages and navigating through screens, which had an ominous tendency to entice the user to a point in the application from which the user could neither advance nor withdraw without professional intervention, has created a generation of computer phobics among the executive decision making cadre.

This psychological barrier was broken when the PC was born or, more properly, when the graphical interface on the PC was made widely available. Now the database should only be a few mouse clicks away and the user can navigate through the application by selecting pictorial icons which have familiar business connotations. No longer is an impressive recall of computer commands required. The combination of a more flexible interface to the data and more powerful database engines to manipulate the data has transformed the possibilities for decision support computing. At the same time these software tools have upped the ante for the software development community since it is no longer adequate to design and present applications logically but it is necessary to design and present them in a manner that is both sympathetic and creative.

There are different estimates of the rate of growth of the data warehouse market. The US-based META Group have forecast that the data warehouse market will grow from $2 billions in 1995 to $8 billions by 1998 and this forecast is accompanied by an additional estimate of the value of the consulting/systems integration market in 1998 at $5 billions. It would appear that the average initial investment by a typical large enterprise in a data warehouse is in the range $4-8 millions. One aspect of the market that is not entirely clear is the extent that small and medium size enterprises will invest heavily in data warehousing because these types of company are not likely to have the same level of data disintegration as the larger enterprises.

Large enterprises have evolved over longer periods, have older systems, have mission-critical operational applications which pre-date modern modelling and documentation standards, and have grown through takeovers and mergers where disparate information systems were never satisfactorily integrated. The smaller enterprise, on the other hand, will have a simpler data architecture based on more integrated application packages which will have built-in reporting facilities. Therefore, the smaller enterprise will not have the same impetus to warehouse data because the enterprise will not have reached a crisis in decision support, but intensive complex marketing strategies by smaller enterprises will still require a separate dedicated data warehouse platform.

The data warehouse is evidence, not of the impact of a new information technology innovation, but of the re-organisation of the existing information technology architecture. It is not a high-risk venture in the sense that the technology is particularly novel or demanding. (There are, to be sure, some technological components missing, but these can be substituted by bespoke software.) The data warehouse project *is* high risk in the sense that the skills required to envision an integrated corporate database and to combine the diverse corporate data structures into an integrated whole will make heavy demands on the skills and competencies of the technical and business partners in the venture. While a degree of commonality will exist in all data warehouse deployments at an architectural level and even at a general strategic level, each data warehouse must be the customised product of the requirements of the particular industry where it is deployed.

The architectural model and the strategic uses for the data warehouse have been presented in this book, but every enterprise which invests in a data warehouse will be solving   its own   particular puzzle. Ultimately the currency of the data warehouse is intellectual rather than technological. This problem will be particularly acute in enterprises which choose to regard the data warehouse as a panacea which will energise their strategy or transform their creaking business processes if these same enterprises have failed to use existing information systems with any degree of ingenuity in the past.

The exploitation of data through the creation and utilisation of applications which use that data to identify patterns which are useful to the business is the mission of the data warehouse.

The potential for the profitable exploitation by business users of the integrated corporate data will be the determining factor for any enterprise considering the data warehouse option. In an era when it is estimated that (in the US) 40% of all commercial capital investment is expended on information systems and when the productivity of service and knowledgeworkers is static or actually in decline it must be conceded that a fundamental problem exists. Most observers have diagnosed the problem as having to do (to a greater or lesser degree) with chronic layers of largely artificial complexity deeply embedded within highly disintegrated functions and structures. If this is the case then the solution will reside somewhere in the agenda for *integration* and *simplification*.

The data warehouse project is an architected response to the deficiencies in the traditionally evolved information systems architecture. It is a means of integrating the islands of computing which have developed into the corporate archipelagos which are a standard feature of the modern enterprise. On each of these islands data will tend not to be logically structured since, in most instances, the primary objective of the system designers will have been to minimise the time taken to process the transaction volumes and thereby keep down the capital cost of the system. While the data will have been structured in a manner which is highly efficient for this purpose it is, more often than not, incomprehensible from the perspective of the business analyst. And there, quite simply, is the problem.

It is precisely because it is the individual business processes that are automated rather than the enterprise as a whole that the objective of integrating the enterprise is occupying so much of the management agenda. This passion for integration can be seen everywhere. It is evident in the attempts by information technology software vendors to offer repository products and CASE tools. It is evident in the attempts of hardware vendors to offer open systems. It is evident in the efforts of industry bodies to develop standards. It is evident too in the ambition of BPR analysts to simplify core business processes and in the efforts of TQM teams on the shop floor to make their environments more coherent. Integration too is the key driver of the data warehouse and the data warehouse complements all of the other initiatives. What differentiates the data warehouse project from the others is that it is not primarily concerned with business processes at all, at least not in the first instance. It is almost implicit in the mind-set of the data warehouse advocate that the existing mess of information systems is a sunk investment by the enterprise and will be around in more-or-less its current state for a long time yet. From this premise flows the assumptions that the comprehensive integration of business processes (and the information systems that support them) is one of life's longer-term aspirations and that it would be too complex, expensive and risky to contemplate anything too ambitious in the short term.

After all, the entire fabric of the enterprise has been woven around the imperfect processes that provide the customer with the product and change will be a painstaking affair. And from there it is a short step to recognise that the integration of data is an achievable short term goal with significant short-term benefits. While this book has cautioned that the data warehouse is not organisationally neutral in its effect, the actual construction and deployment of a data warehouse does not necessitate (for most enterprises) any dramatic organisational adjustment. This is the real attraction of the data warehouse for many of the early adopters. It provides a quick hit in a marketplace where superior strategy has the potential to be rewarded.

Superior strategy is going to be a key driver of the data warehouse phenomenon. In a survey of data warehouse implementations in Europe [25] the key enablers of data warehousing were as identified as 'user demand' and 'changing business markets". Over 71% of those surveyed identified business drivers as enablers of the data warehouse project. These same organisations identified the key inhibitors to be predominantly organisational. While technology was seen to be a key ingredient in the data warehouse project it was not seen to be either a key inhibitor or enabler. This is clear evidence, if evidence were needed, that data warehousing is about the business, not about technology.

In the past decade, products have proliferated at an astonishing pace. It is a trend that can be observed in every industry sector and in every category of consumer goods and service. Most enterprises are pursuing business strategies based on line extensions rather than product expansion. Organisations clearly see line extensions and 'versioning' of products as a way of growing turnover. Of course, this strategy only works if the enterprise can target micro-segments and design product lines around the clear needs of identifiable markets. Here there is enormous opportunity for data to be shared (or traded) between producers and retailers. The retailers are likely to further strengthen their hold over suppliers through the use of data about customer buying patterns. The pharmacies will capture the data that the pharmaceutical companies need. The book-stores will have the data that the publishers need. The clothing stores will have the data that the garment industry needs. What this will mean for industry at large is unclear, but customer behaviour data patterns are going to become so important to the survival of companies that producers may rethink their present business model, and seek to have some control over the channels for their products.

One of the more interesting data co-relations that Wal-Mart discovered was that two specific products were purchased by the same type of customer at the same time of the day. The products in question are diapers and beer. The time of day was 6 p.m. The customer was a male on the way home from work. (Obviously, he is told to get one item, and decides on impulse to get the other). When this trend was identified Wal-Mart stocked the beer on the shelves next to the diapers. The volume of beer sales doubled. But this is run-of-the-mill data warehousing. What Wal-Mart have now done is to take the data warehouse project one stage further. Wal-Mart have recognised the importance of giving their suppliers access to the data. They have handed over stock control of some of the products that they stock to their major suppliers. So now Procter & Gamble can see how many diapers are sold; what varieties are sold and where their products are best positioned. These advanced data warehouse implementation clearly demonstrate that data will provide a basis for a different kind of relationship between supplier and retailer.

And many enterprises which have enthusiastically deployed data warehouse applications recognise that their existing business processes are imperfect and will require planned change in the medium and long term. But they also recognise that the existing processes are often well capable of supporting new strategies which can provide short-term competitive advantage to the enterprise. The early adopters also recognise that when they do move to optimise their operational business processes, that the re-engineering of these processes should be based on a corporate strategy that is derived from a sound empirical analysis of data.

The objective of the data warehouse is to capture data, and then to exploit that data. The goal is to harvest knowledge for the enterprise. The final task is to apply that knowledge.

References

1. Drucker, P. (1983) The coming of the new organisation. *Harvard Business Review,* Jan/Feb.

2. Hopper, M. D. (1990) *Harvard Business Review,* May/June.

3. Eysenck, M. W. and Keane, M. T. (1990) *Cognitive Psychology,* Lawrence Erlbaum, Hove.

4. de Bono, E. (1969) *The Mechanism of Mind,* Jonathan Cape, London.

5. de Bono, E. (1990) *Masterthinkers Handbook,* Penguin, Harmondsworth.

6. Chin, R. and Benne, K. (1976) General strategies for effecting changes in human systems in W. G. Bennis, K. D. Benne, R. Chin, and K. E. Coren (eds) *The Planning of Change,* Holt, Rienhart & Winston, New York.

7. Ibid p. 23.

8. Festinger, L. (1957) *A Theory of Cognitive Dissonance,* Stanford University Press.

9. Aronson, E. (1988) *The Social Animal,* 5th edn, W. H. Freeman, p. 124.

10. Silver, M.S. (1991) *Systems that Support Decision Making,* John Wiley, Chichester.

11. Simon, H. (1960) *The New Science of Management Decision,* Harper & Row New York.

12. Anthony, R. (1965) Planning and control systems, *Harvard Business School.*

13. Gorry, G. A. and Scott-Morton, M. S. (1971) A framework for management information systems, *Sloane Management Review.*

14. Gorry, G. A. and Scott-Morton M. S. (1989) *Sloane Management Review.*

15. Silver, M. S. (1991) *Systems that Support Decision Making,* John Wiley, Chichester.

16. Ibid.

17. Zani, W. (1970) Blueprint for MIS, *Harvard Business Review,* Nov/Dec.

18 Davis, S. M. (1987) *Future Perfect*, Addison-Wesley, Reading, MA.

19. *Financial Times*, 24th June 1993, p. 15.

20 Davis, S. M. (1987) *Future Perfect*, Addison-Wesley, Reading, MA.

21. McKenna, R. (1991) Marketing is Everything, *Harvard Business Review,* Jan/Feb.

22. Simon, H. A. (1960) *The New Science of Management Decision*, Harper & Row, New York.

23. Glazer, R. (1993) Measuring the value of data: the information intensive organisation, *IBM Systems Journal*, **32**, (1), 99 – 110.

24. Nolan, B. and Norton T. (1974) Managing the four stages of EDP growth, *Harvard Business Review*, Jan/Feb.

25. *Data Warehouse Network*, DRUID Survey, 1995.

Index

The Data Warehouse Network

*The Data Warehouse Network developed from informal
beginnings when small numbers of early adopters of this
technology began to make contact across Europe and North
America. The Network now has a large number of affiliates including
consultants, user organisations and vendor organisations. The Network
and maintains a full time office and research centre in Ireland.*

- ◆ **Mission**
  The Mission of the Data Warehouse Network is to provide
  and maintain an independent forum for data warehouse
  developers. The Network is dedicated to the development and
  delivery of high-quality support services in the form
  of research, consultancy, information and education.

- ◆ **Independent**
  The Data Warehouse Network is entirely independent
  of any other organisation, including vendor and supplier
  organisations. All work conducted by the network is
  guided by the highest standards of independence, impartiality,
  integrity, and fairness.

- ◆ **Publications**
  The Data Warehouse Network published a quarterly journal
  which discusses the emerging issues and trends in data
  warehousing as well as a monthly newsletter. In addition
  the Network publishes specialised reports, including product
  evaluations and surveys.

- ◆ **Contact**
  The Data Warehouse Network can be contacted at:
  P.O. Box 7, Skibbereen, Cork, Ireland.
  Telephone +353+28+38483
  Facsimile +353+28+38485